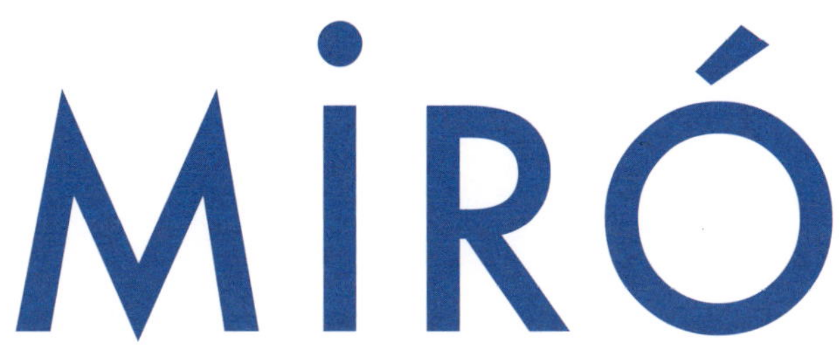

THE EXPERIENCE OF SEEING

LATE WORKS, 1963–1981

Carmen Fernández Aparicio • Belén Galán Martín • Charles Palermo
Pere Portabella • Jesús Carrillo

Published by the Seattle Art Museum in collaboration with the Museo Nacional Centro de Arte Reina Sofía
and in association with Yale University Press, New Haven and London

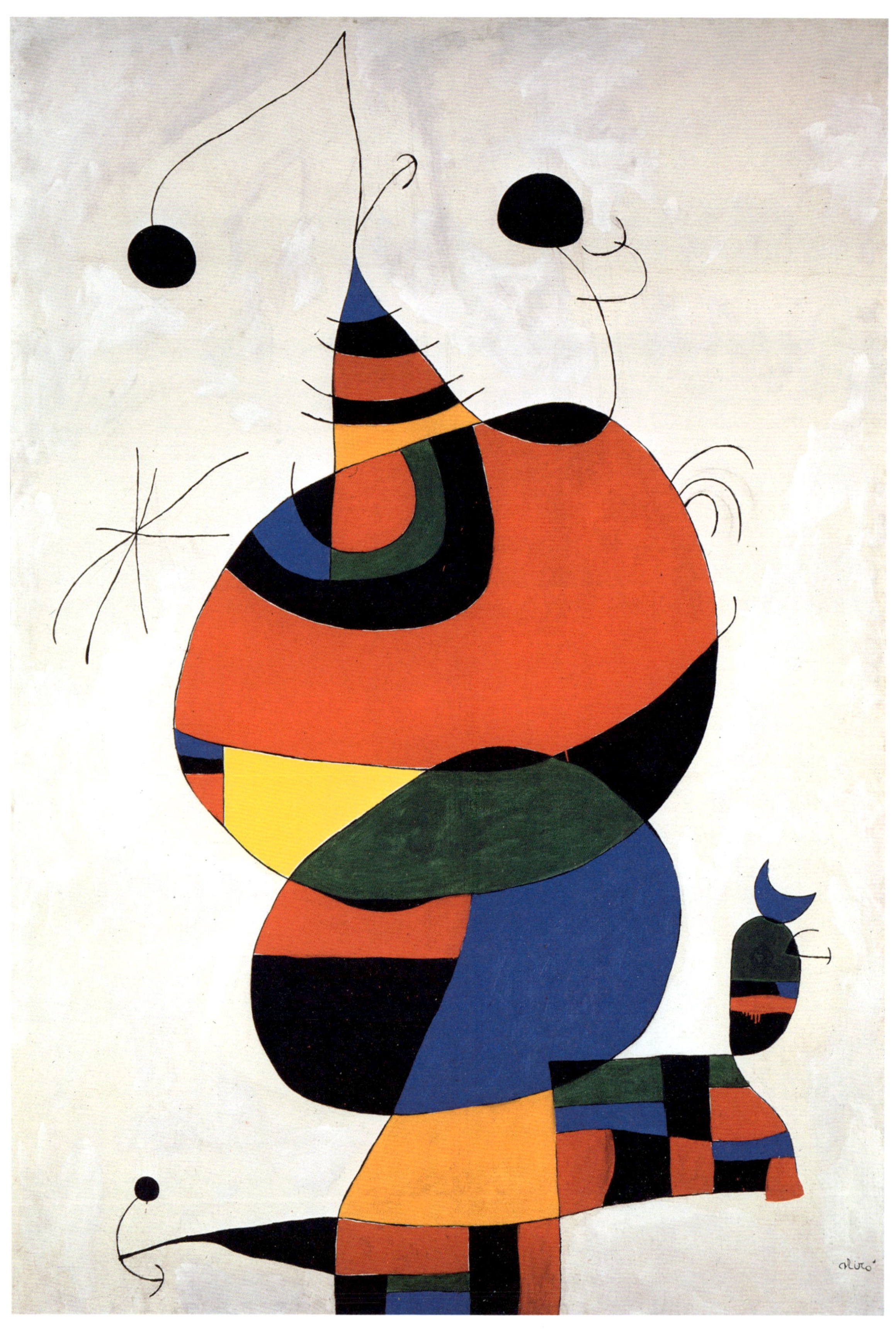

Mujer, pájaro y estrella (Homenaje a Picasso) (Woman, Bird and Star [Homage to Picasso])
February 15, 1966 / April 3–8, 1973, oil on canvas, 96 7/16 × 66 15/16 in. (245 × 170 cm)

From the Ministry of Education, Culture, and Sport, Spain

The Museo Reina Sofía's obligation to its viewers and the public nature of its collections have allowed for the creation of myriad narratives and events extending far beyond the institution's walls. Events such as the mounting of exhibitions at external venues are made possible entirely and with great skill thanks to the cooperation of entities and institutions that have been steadfast in their promotion of legacies such as Miró's. Their support has made it possible for the artist's work to reach audiences outside Spain.

The Seattle Art Museum has committed itself to *Miró: The Experience of Seeing*, which showcases a broad selection of works by the painter from Barcelona. These works have been chosen from among the wide representation of his creations in the Museo Reina Sofía's collection. This selection presents us with an opportunity to become familiar with what is probably one of the least known and at the same time richest periods of the Barcelonese artist's oeuvre. This carefully selected and curated exhibition creates a conversation among the painting, sculpture, and films of a period that spans the 1960s and 1970s.

On the journey through the exhibition halls that host this selection, just as through the pages of the present volume, many visitors will recognize Miró's personal language, which has been transformed into a landmark of the art that gave rise to modernity. At the same time, visitors will have an opportunity to discover *Miró the Other* (such is the title of one of the films by Pere Portabella that appears in the exhibition), which exists in conversation with a time quite different from the one in which the artist's career was born.

It is of particular importance that this exhibition was made possible by two events that are connected across time; both are related to the implication of civil society with respect to cultural institutions. First is the decision by Miró's heirs to donate his bequest, which at the Museum's outset greatly enriched what was to become one of Europe's most distinguished public collections. Second, we would like to recognize the inestimable involvement of and work accomplished by the Seattle Art Museum in presenting a selection of the aforementioned bequest in its galleries. Both deeds are living proof of the institutional and civic determination to promote culture and heritage, and both will undoubtedly find affirmation in the public's response to the presentation of this group of Miró's mature works.

Directors' Foreword

Kimerly Rorschach & Manuel J. Borja-Villel

This exhibition presents a rare opportunity to introduce American audiences to the astounding and innovative paintings and sculptures that Joan Miró created in his later years. Drawn from the collection of the Museo Nacional Centro de Arte Reina Sofía in Madrid, it is the first exhibition dedicated to this fruitful period in the artist's life in the United States. Although there have been numerous surveys and retrospectives dedicated to Miró's work in other parts of the country, there has not been a comprehensive exhibition of Miró's work on the West Coast, making this a particularly meaningful undertaking for both our institutions.

Miró: The Experience of Seeing focuses on Miró's late period, a chapter that even today remains mostly overshadowed by his artistic contributions during the interwar and immediate postwar periods. In the 1960s and 1970s, Miró wrestled with his own symbols. He found himself constantly struggling against traditional historiographies, which attempted to freeze his figure into an icon of an earlier time.

The story of this exhibition begins in the 1960s. Miró can be seen as a figure that quietly spans two generations of artists: one looked to him as the father of a "signic language," the basis for the prevailing pictorial tendencies following the Second World War, including Abstract Expressionism. His influence also spread, even more indirectly, to some of the Spanish artists who, not long after, would join the "paradigm shift" that took place in the arts during the sixties and which signaled the rise of Conceptual art. Among these artists is Pere Portabella, whose films engage in a dialog with Miró's works in this exhibition, and who provides an example of Miro's late interest in new media and younger generations of artists.

This exhibition is possible thanks to the Museo Reina Sofía's policies promoting the international diffusion of its collections, which have been fundamental for the institution. In this way the collection has been able to reach new audiences, such as in this case that of the Seattle Art Museum. The two institutions have combined forces and undertaken this task to promote an international dialog between the invisible commonalities on both sides of the Atlantic. This conversation will generate new ways of seeing and so give new meaning to this segment of the Museo Reina Sofía's distinguished collection.

Miró: The Experience of Seeing was conceived by Chief Curator of Sculpture Carmen Fernández Aparicio and Chief Curator of Paintings Belén Galán Martín, under the guidance of Rosario Peiró, Chief Curator of the permanent collection at the Museo Reina Sofía. We would like to express our gratitude to the curators' fresh perspective on Miró's late work, as their expertise and research introduce the artist in a compelling new way. We are extremely grateful to Pere Portabella for providing this opportunity to frame Miró's work with two of his films. We would also like to thank the catalog contributors, Carmen Fernández Aparicio; Charles Palermo, Alumni Memorial Term Distinguished Associate Professor of Art History at the College of William and Mary; Jesús Carrillo; and Pere Portabella, for their unique contributions.

Our sincerest gratitude goes to Miró's family for their willingness to assist in all activities concerning the artist. Additionally, we like to think of Luis Fernando Esteban, the Honorary Consul of Spain in Seattle, as the patron saint of this exhibition. His untiring advocacy for artistic and cultural exchange between Seattle and Spain opened the doors for this collaboration, a first for our respective museums—and we hope the first of many. Miguel Ángel Cortés, member of the Spanish parliament and board member of the Museo Reina Sofía, generously hosted several early gatherings that facilitated a lively exchange of ideas that led to this collaboration.

Since much of this work by Miró is little known outside of Europe, we are very pleased that this important exhibition will travel to Durham, North Carolina, and Denver, Colorado, allowing audiences in other parts of the country to see it. For this, we would like to express our gratitude to our fellow museum directors, Sarah Schroth, Mary D. B.T. and James H. Semans Director at the Nasher Museum of Art at Duke University, and Christoph Heinrich, Frederick and Jan Mayer Director at the Denver Art Museum, who recognized the significance of this exhibition and collaborated with us to bring it to their museums.

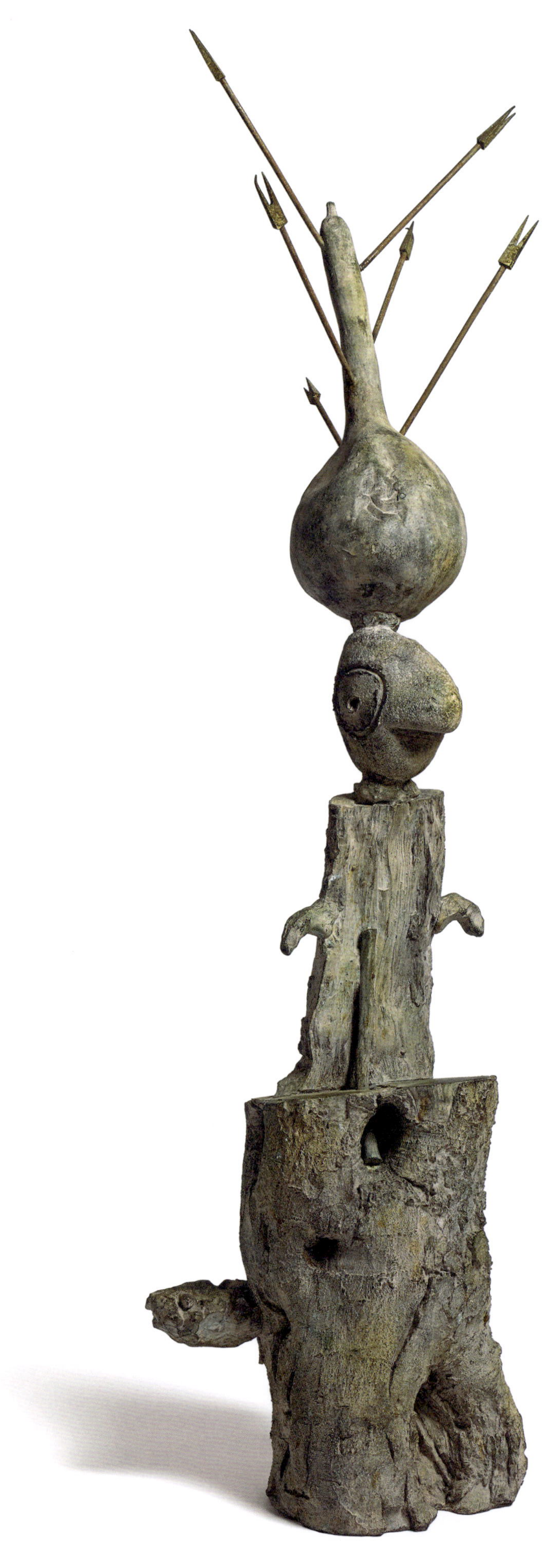

An international undertaking of this kind requires substantial financial heft. The exhibition is supported in all three venues by an indemnity from the Federal Council on the Arts and the Humanities. The Seattle presentation and related programs are made possible with critical funding provided by the Seattle Art Museum's Fund for Special Exhibitions. This fund is driven by a committed group of forward-thinking donors and allows the museum to bring exceptional exhibitions to Seattle. Early support for this exhibition came from our corporate sponsor, Christie's, for which we are most grateful. Thank you to the Seattle Art Museum Supporters, the museum's auxiliary fundraising group, for dedicating support to this exhibition. Additional funds are provided by Washington State Arts Commission / National Endowment for the Arts and the Herman and Faye Sarkowsky Endowment. *Miro: The Experience of Seeing* is further supported by a generous group of donors in honor of Bagley Wright.

Thanks to the initiative of our museum trustee Curtis Wong and his dedication to creating new tools for learning and interpretation, the Seattle Art Museum is delighted to receive additional support for interpretive technology from Microsoft Research's Rich Interactive Narratives technology in collaboration with Brown University's Touch Art Gallery Team.

Figure
1969
Patinated bronze
55⅞ × 16¾ × 16⁵⁄₁₆ in.
(142 × 42.5 × 41.5 cm)

Our very special thanks goes to the Seattle Art Museum's senior staff and their teams, who, with their customary expertise and flair, have coordinated this exhibition and all related programs. We are especially grateful to Chiyo Ishikawa, our Susan Brotman Deputy Director for Art and Curator of European Painting and Sculpture, and to Catharina Manchanda, Jon and Mary Shirley Curator of Modern and Contemporary Art, who headed our curatorial team on this project. They were assisted by Carrie Dedon, Modern & Contemporary Art Curatorial Assistant; Megan Peterson, Exhibitions Coordinator; and Gabriela Ayala, Special Projects Intern, to whom we are also very grateful.

We hope that the exhibition will inspire both seasoned admirers of Miró and a new generation of art enthusiasts to see the artist and his work in a new light. Long admired in the United States, Miró's work will now be more fully understood and appreciated here.

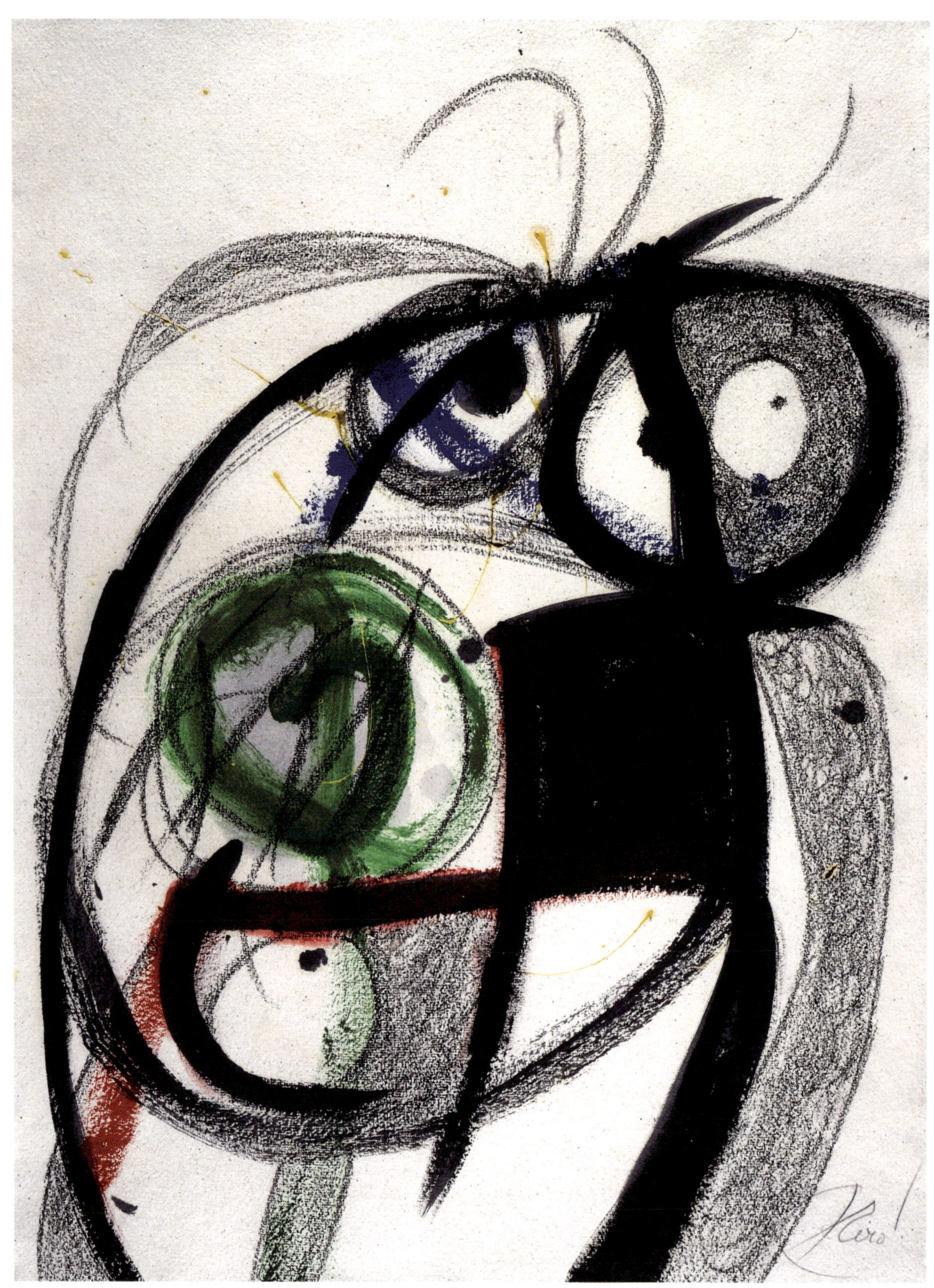

Curators' Statement

Carmen Fernández Aparicio & Belén Galán Martín

This exhibition project, run by the Museo Reina Sofía Collections Department, centers around works from the final years of Joan Miró (1893–1983), a time when the circumstances in Miró's life and art meant he could make a fundamental change in direction. In 1956, Miró moved to a new studio in Son Abrines, Mallorca, designed by Josep Lluís Sert. In his studio-home he could, for the first time, gather together the entirety of his production, meaning he now had direct access to all his works and could revise and rethink as he wished. This meant that from then on his work was fuelled by a rereading of his artistic experience, the result of which was a complete break with the hierarchization of artistic signs and absolute freedom of expression. His works during those mature years represent a more personal language, where neither painting nor sculpture takes precedence. Instead, approaching these disciplines again from his original perspective, he set out to explore their conceptual limits by questioning their very nature.

From that moment on, Miró, who had been at the very center of the evolution of the modern art connected to the Parisian avant-garde since the 1920s, began a process of introspection, through which he arrived at the utmost simplification of his universe. The starting point for his work at this time was an accidental or fortuitous motif—something as simple as a smudge, a drop of paint, a fingerprint, a found object or something from nature—which became the initial push toward re-creating a common subject in his work: the representation of nature and the human figure. Miró goes beyond reality as a referent in order to transmute it into material and signs, constructing an essential symbolic language that he uses to solve visual problems.

Personnage (Figure)
1977
India ink, acrylic, gouache, and tempera on Barker paper
30¹¹⁄₁₆ × 22¹³⁄₁₆ in.
(78 × 58 cm)

The paintings and sculptures in the exhibition closely examine aspects of the art-making process, part of the basis of his output since his earliest works. In his quest to transcend the idea of easel painting, the pictorial space is enlarged across expanded canvas fields, on which calligraphic signs reach maximum intensity through minimum resources, reflecting the artist's attempt to reach a square one of painting through simplicity and emptiness. Assembling found objects, and adding techniques such as modelling and bronze casting, also meant that he could create a work that somehow bestrode all of modern sculpture's possibilities for expression.

Without ever being part of any formal categories, Miró continually changed his expressive medium, developing a process of intervention-reaction in the various series that he worked on for extensive periods. The modifications he introduced affected the group's final equilibrium, always reiterating in both media the same conceptual aspects and technical solutions: simplicity, flatness, line, gesture, and ideogram.

This anti-drawing, objectual creation of Miró's reveals the genesis of his work and its connection to close observation of nature, which was so clear during this final period. In it, he repeats the representation of woman (Earth Mother), a ritual image going back thousands of years and the most common figure in Mallorcan folk sculpture typology, and other motifs connected to the heavens and the landscape, now lending this subject matter a certain universality. This aspect is connected to Miró's desire to go beyond traditional artistic basics in order to get past object-painting-sculpture, by grasping the experience as a whole.

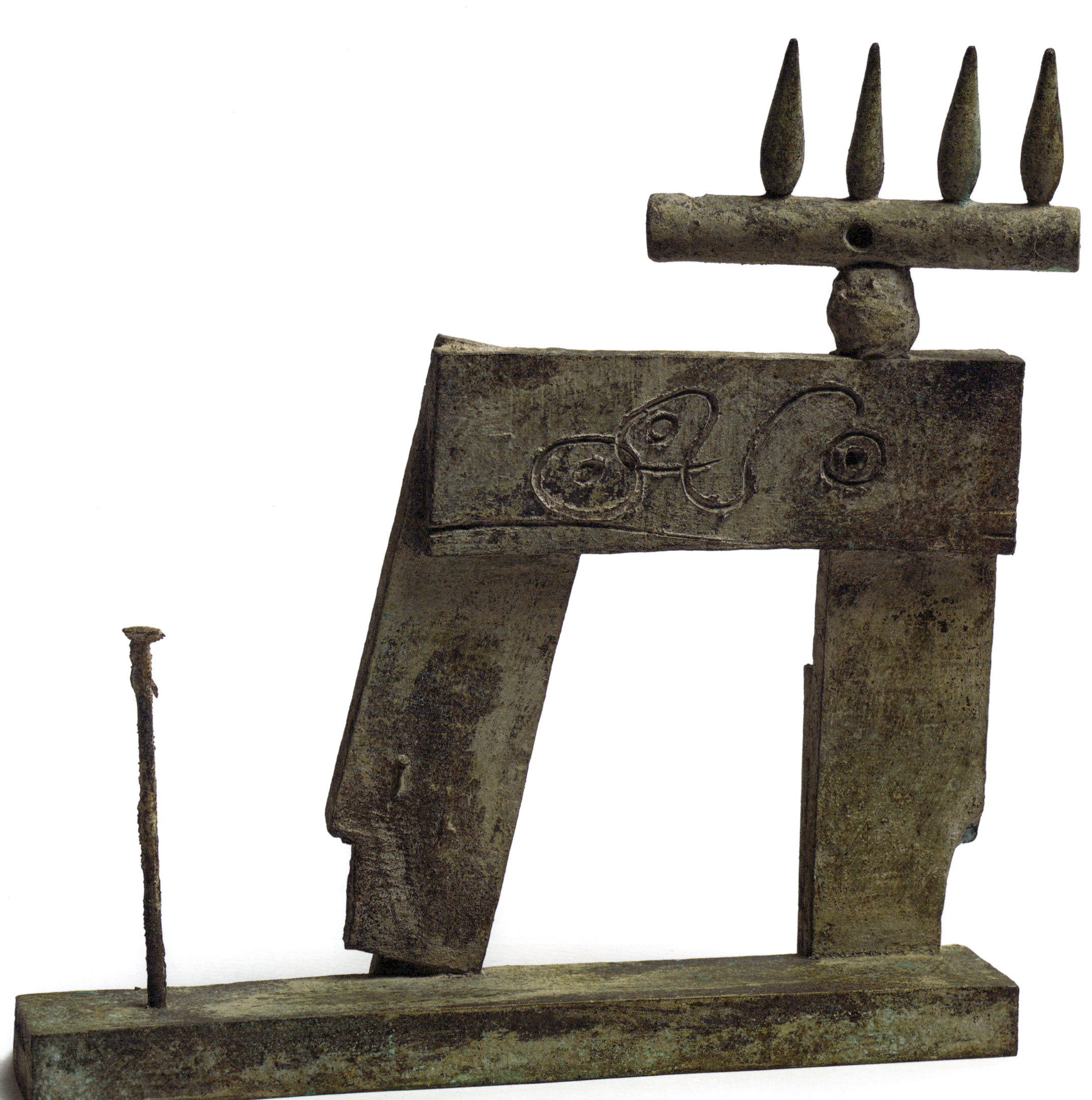

In Conversation

Jesús Carrillo & Pere Portabella

Joan Miró played a singular role in Catalan culture in the waning years of the Franco dictatorship. After spending more than a decade in reclusion on Mallorca, he began to pay sporadic visits to Barcelona, and these encounters, despite the artist's timid nature, stirred up the encumbering layers of a cultural life that was struggling to step out of the shadows imposed by the regime and find its own identity. During the sixties and seventies Joan Miró managed to maintain his independence both in relationship to all efforts to assimilate him to the official culture, as well as the tendency toward mythification by a society in search of points of reference. Joan Miró was never a passive object of these maneuvers. Rather, in the attitudes and positions he staked out, he made clear to the end the role he wanted to play at every stage. In this context his encounter with a militant young filmmaker, Pere Portabella, would be paradigmatic, sparking an intense dialog between two generations separated by the Franco regime: the prewar avant-garde, on the one hand, and the increasingly radical neo-vanguard that arose in the final years of the dictatorship.

Jesús Carrillo—The meeting between the iconic figure of Catalan culture in the waning years of the Franco dictatorship, known for his uncompromising character, and Pere Portabella, an iconoclastic filmmaker in the turbulent late sixties, could have been a clash of incomprehension. However, from the outset there was a profound mutual understanding and partnership. In what terms and by what means did this encounter take place?

Jeune fille (Young Girl)
1967
Patinated bronze
13 × 14³⁄₁₆ × 2¾ in.
(33 × 36 × 7 cm)

Pere Portabella—My first meeting with Joan Miró took place in the hat shop of Joan Prats,[1] thanks to the poet Joan Brossa, as well as Arnau Puig, and Antoni Tàpies[2] in the mid fifties, when Miró began to visit Barcelona more frequently.

Joan Prats and the Sala Gaspar, the gallery Miró worked with, would be the main bridges between Miró and the city in that first period. Miró received us cordially and proved very receptive throughout a long and wide-ranging conversation that covered a number of topics. There was an immediate empathy between the painter from Palma and a member of a generation that was trying to link linguistic transgression with political action. For me it was the beginning of a long friendship and professional collaboration that lasted until his death. This relationship, though not continuous, was intense and generous on his end, leading to encounters and artistic, social, and political collaborations that Miró considered just and appropriate. For instance, he offered to design, for the newly established trade union Comisiones Obreras [Workers' Commissions], a poster for the 1968 May Day celebration.[3] I also remember when, inspired by another emblematic figure, the architect Josep Lluís Sert, who had just returned from exile, he signed a letter supporting the demands of a group I belonged to, Democratic Assemblies against the Dictatorship.

The collaboration between the two of us took shape in three short films we made for the exhibition and homage to the work and person of Joan Miró, organized by the Col·legi Oficial d'Arquitectes de Catalunya i Balears [Official College of Architects of Catalonia and the Balearic Islands] in 1969. This was in response to the exhibition that the Franco regime had sponsored the year before in a futile attempt to make Miró part of the institutional culture.

J.C. At that time, culture, design, architecture, and art would become the arena in which the different images of Catalan modernity were struggling for dominance. What role did your generation attribute to the mythical figures of the avant-garde in general and to Miró specifically?

P.P. For us, Pablo Picasso, the filmmaker Luis Buñuel, and particularly Miró were identified with prewar modernity and the avant-garde spirit. We understood their presence and partnership with us as an important support for our revolutionary impulses.

I remember the performance of the *Concert irregular* at the Maeght Foundation in June 1968,[4] with music by Carles Santos and lyrics by Joan Brossa, for which I designed the set. It was an homage to Joan Miró for his seventy-fifth birthday, and it became not only one of the most revolutionary avant-garde statements of the time but also a clear political position for Catalan culture. At one point in the piece—a protest against the Vietnam War—the authorities in attendance stood up and stomped out, while the rest of the audience sat motionless to the end.

A few years before, in 1960, in response to my invitation from the Selection Committee of the Cannes Film Festival to participate in the presentation of my first production, Carlos Saura's film *Los golfos* (*The Delinquents*), an extraordinary thing occurred when happenstance and blind luck conspired to bring us face-to-face with Luis Buñuel in the hotel lobby. The consequences of this chance encounter are well known.

I would become the producer of *Viridiana* and the following year, in 1961, we won the Palme d'Or for best film. Even better was the media scandal that beset the Franco regime when they were denounced in the official Vatican newspaper, *L'Osservatore Romano*, for having authorized such a sacrilegious and libelous monstrosity. This was another failed attempt by the dictatorship to manipulate the figure of Luis Buñuel. The film was declared nonexistent, Buñuel's identity as a Spaniard was denied, along with an implicit threat of excommunication for which, by the way, I'm still waiting. Another attempt by the regime to cover up its shameful behavior.

In this brief period I was able to go to both Cannes and Mougins to visit Picasso. These were critical years for me. Three iconic figures [Picasso, Buñuel, and Miró] salvaged from political and artistic exile in the full flush of their creativity, unquestioned reference points in opposition to the dictatorship. They agreed on many aspects of the passionate search for codes and narratives that, as Miró declared, "assassinate painting" in search of freedom by going down the path of transgression and political insubordination.

Given his example it's no wonder that in the sixties I was integrated, or embedded, into the politically most radical poetic theorization.

J.C. But Miró didn't just resonate with the imagination of young radicals, he also became a touchstone for Catalan culture in general.

P.P. Clearly we weren't the only ones looking to Miró at that time. From elementary schools to furniture design tied to the Eina School,[5] the Miró spirit was adopted as a mark of Catalanism and modernity, which were difficult to tell apart then. The image of Barcelona promoted by local institutions also aspired to reflect that spirit of modernity through commissions like the murals in the Barcelona El Prat airport and the Pla del l'Os, and the sculpture *Woman and Bird* in Escorxador Park. The Franco government even tried to appropriate Miró as part of its strategy to clean up its image at a time when the artist was becoming one of the most highly recognized figures of the historic avant-garde, acclaimed by international critics and collectors.

J.C. What was Miró's response to the interest shown in him from so many different quarters?

P.P. Miró had the virtue of total autonomy. His reserved personality was a safeguard against public overexposure. He was not very accessible and avoided the spotlight, taking refuge in long periods of silence and ambiguous gestures, but at close range in my experience our relationship was open and flowing. His barely contained radicalism exuded a passionate energy that swept others up. He was interested in collective endeavors and most of all had respect for the work of artisans. The artist, in his estimation, had to make an effort to abandon, reject, shed individuality, to sink into anonymity. This attitude allowed him to take part judiciously in those processes of Barcelona culture that interested him, which were quite a few. Miró was a regular at the Club 49, a focal point for vanguard culture and contemporary music, where we all gathered. Strangely, despite this penchant for modernity and the avant-garde, Miró's interest gravitated toward popular culture, the giant and big-headed puppets (*gigantes y cabezudos*), the Procession of the Virgin, and the *calçotadas*.[6]

Despite his relationship with and respect for the visual artists, he would strengthen his connection with the world of dance, theater, and film, fields in which he found the most driven members of the young cultural scene in Barcelona.

J.C. His relationship with the highly politicized Catalan and Spanish cultural life in those years made him take a public stance against the Franco regime. You were both witness and active participant on several of those occasions.

P.P. The year 1969 began with the government's declaration in January of a state of emergency. Just a few days earlier the filmmaker Juan Antonio Bardem, the painter Juan Genovés, the art critic José María Moreno Galván, and I myself appeared before the Ministry of the Interior to submit a document denouncing instances of torture, mistreatment, and imprisonment without habeas corpus of political prisoners, addressed directly to the minister, General Camilo Alonso Vega.

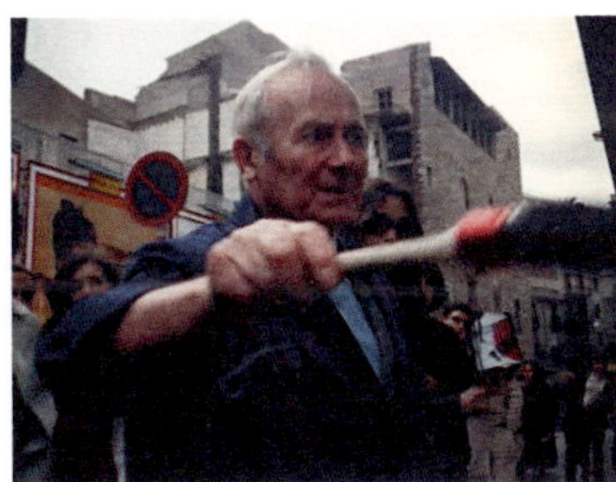

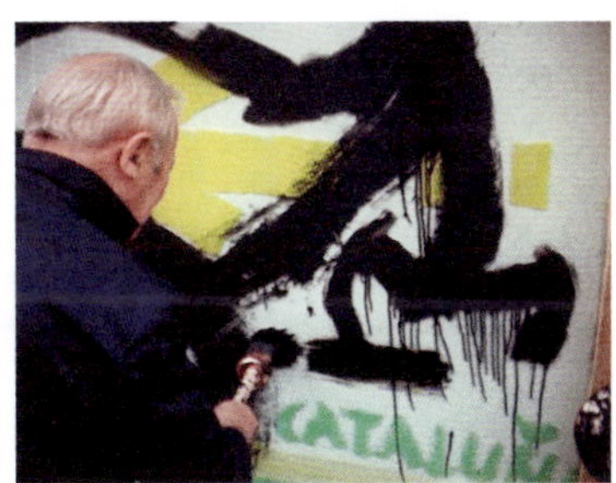

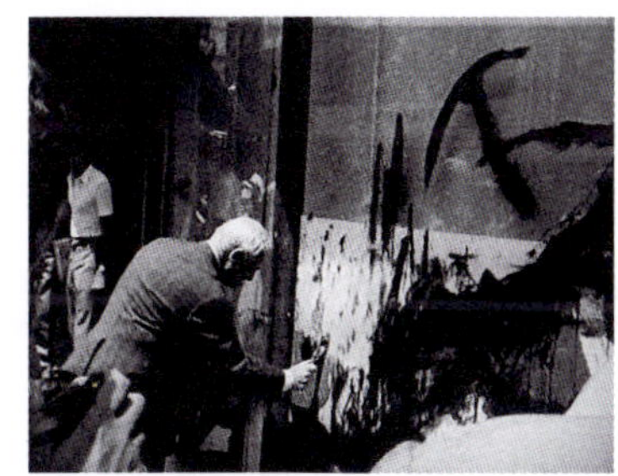

Film stills from Pere Portabella, *Miró l'altre (Miró the Other)*, 1969. 16 mm film, b/w and color, sound; 15 min. Films 59.

His chief of staff called us in, a *guardia civil* neatly dressed in an impeccable uniform, with a sharp crease in his freshly pressed trousers. Most impressive. I'll forgo the tense conversation. In response to our question about when we would receive an answer, since the minister refused to meet with us: "Don't worry, it will be very soon." Indeed it was. The next day, on my return from Madrid, Miró, Tàpies, Antonio Saura, and Jacques Dupin were waiting for me in a restaurant in the Barceloneta.[7] The media had already reported, giving our full names, that we were responsible for the attack on the honor of the Armed Forces, for slandering the Civil Guard, and for offending the fatherland. I was subpoenaed to appear in Madrid before the Attorney General, where I received treatment as exquisite in form as it was brutal in content. That's how the year began.

At the end of the next year, due to his involvement in the protests against the Burgos trials (Proceso de Burgos),[8] Miró would again stand up to the Franco regime. I was chosen, along with a representative of the Consell de Forças Politicas [Council of Political Forces], to deliver to General Díez Alegría, head of the Joint Chiefs of Staff of the Armed Forces, with the intervention of José María de Areilza, a signed document demanding that the accused face a civil trial instead of the court martial, among other demands, including the abolition of the death penalty. The general urged me to set the document on his desk without opening it, and we conversed at length. If he had opened it then, he would have found Miró's signature heading the list of demands and he might have had to arrest us and put us all on trial, including Joan Miró.

On our return to Barcelona a sit-in of three hundred intellectuals, artists, and professionals was being planned for December 11 in the Monastery of Montserrat to bring pressure on the regime and mobilize international public opinion, demanding the abolition of the death penalty and the annulment of the court martial. Shortly before the sit-in began Miró and his wife appeared, together with Tàpies, in support of the protest. They were greeted with a standing ovation. In a meeting I attended it was decided to ask the assembly to excuse Miró and Tàpies from participating in the sit-in before the police surrounded the monastery for two days, which in fact they did.

J.C. Can you explain in this context the 1969 exhibition in the College of Architects in Barcelona and the proposal to film the destruction of the murals Miró painted on the façade?

P.P. At that time I was an active member of the Anti-Franco Unitary roundtable. And I was getting ready to film *Vampir-Cuadecuc*. At this point in the sixties Opus Dei[9] rushed in with an attempt to better the image of the regime in a context of timid advances in cultural and economic policy. To this end they organized a Miró exhibit in Barcelona in order to exploit his name, just as they had done with Luis Buñuel. This was the first official exhibit of his work. As I mentioned before, at the last minute they opened the show without the presence of Miró, who was in Barcelona but refused to attend.

A year later, the Official College of Architects of Catalonia and the Balearic Islands, at the request of a group of young architects, proposed to give a resounding response to the official exhibit, denouncing the manipulation of the painter's name, who on this occasion lent his full support and cooperation to the project. I was a member of the Interdisciplinary Committee, which commissioned me to make three short films to screen during the exhibit. Miró proposed painting the ground floor windows of the College of Architects as a way of publicizing the exhibit. My charge was to shoot a documentary on the painting of the mural. My immediate response was that I had no interest in making a documentary, for to be honest there were others who could do it better. A few hours later I called to propose shooting the painting of the mural on the condition that on the very day the exhibit closed, I would also film the destruction of the mural by Miró's own hand.

This was the only way that made sense to film the painting. As far as I was concerned, this would bring out the importance of the process and the ephemeral nature of the action itself. Faced with the tension this created among the radicals who were opposed to my idea, I decided to propose it directly to Joan Miró. And that's what happened. He immediately agreed. Miró was definitive when he recalled the event: "It was necessary to do it this way." It was an extraordinary moment of connection between the two of us, in the radical subversion that tied in with the dynamics of the conceptual art of the time.

Early on the morning of April 28 Miró appeared, wearing a shopkeeper's smock, to paint the forty-four meters of windows of the College of Architects, with a broom in one hand and a housepainter's brush in the other.

Two months later, one midday toward the end of June, Miró himself, spatula in hand and I with a camera, began the operation of destroying the mural. Truth be told, we had the invaluable help of the janitorial staff, who finished the task with professional competence, leaving no trace of the mural (ill. p. 13).

At this point in the story I must quote Miró when he said, "I need to work slowly with the professional dignity of an old workman, for only in this way will I achieve the beauty and consistency of the material."

J.C. The process of labor, the artisan's laboratory, are part of Joan Miró's iconography as an artist; nonetheless, in your documentary the singular figure and only protagonist is the anonymous work itself. What is the meaning of that displacement?

P.P. For my part, I understood the singularity of the contribution of artisans when they occupy a nontransferable space in the process of concretion of the aesthetic materiality of the artist's original idea. That's why in my two films, *Miró Tapestry* and *Miró the Forge* from 1974, Miró's presence would have made no sense. Incidentally, on that fateful September 11, 2001, the tapestry was hanging in the lobby of one of the Twin Towers in New York. Finally, it's all about the complexity of contemporary creativity and the artist's social and political responsibility.

J.C. Your relationship would not be limited to your interest in establishing a dialog with the artist and his work, but also it would produce a process in the opposite direction, where Miró was the one who moved closer to the filmmaker's trade.

P.P. A warm sense of closeness and approachability emanated from Miró's sensitivity, as I had the opportunity to experience on numerous occasions. In 1972 I asked him to make a poster for my film *Umbracle* (before that, Tàpies made the poster for *No contéis con los dedos* and Joan Ponç the one for *Vampir-Cuadecuc*). Miró immediately asked me to write down the title of the film in capital letters. A little while later Joan Gaspar, Miró's gallery agent in Barcelona, called to tell me that the poster was ready. When I picked it up at the gallery, Gaspar pointed out that the word Umbracle was missing the *A*, and that I would have to let Miró know so he could correct it, though it would be a nuisance for him. I looked at the poster: there was nothing to let Miró know about. The *A* was hidden, suspended above the title like a bird in flight. On that occasion Miró not only painted the poster but also had the gallery owner print fifty lithographs, signed and numbered for sale, on the condition that 50 percent of the sales would go to me. That my financial situation for producing my films was precarious was no secret. Thanks to this I was able to pay my debts and finish the films with no difficulty.

The shooting of *Miró Tapestry* and *Miró the Forge* gave rise to long conversations in which I remember he gave me his impressions of the landscape of his youth in Mont-roig. I suggested that he write a film script just based on what he was telling me about the country house. At first he was concerned, because he didn't know what was involved in writing a screenplay. I gave him some guidelines about sequencing and with them he produced a screenplay on six sheets of paper, which later I enlarged to one meter to be hung as a picture, coming full circle from film to painting.

TRANSLATED BY ANTHONY L. GEIST

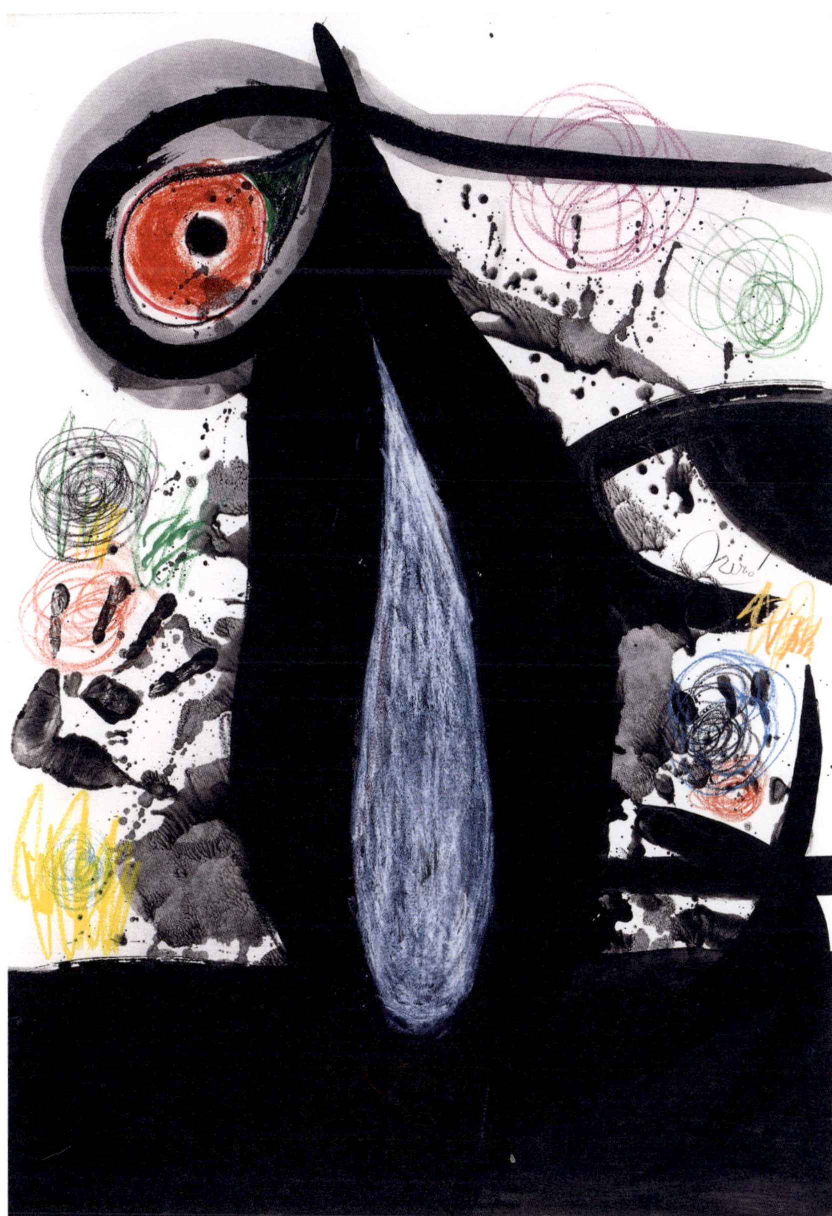

Femme, personnage, oiseau (Woman, Figure, Bird)
1973–77
India ink, wash, wax, and graphite pencil on Arches paper
35¼ × 24¹³⁄₁₆ in. (89.5 × 63 cm)

Detail on pp. 16–17.

NOTES

Explanatory notes by Carmen Fernández Aparicio

1. Joan Prats (Barcelona, 1881–1970) was a friend of Miró's from their early years; in 1915 they both participated in the drawing sessions of the Cercle Artistic de Saint Lluc and together discovered the avant-garde art that the Galeria Dalmau in Barcelona featured in those years.

Prats played an important role in the introduction of the artistic avant-garde in Catalonia in the prewar period, when he founded the ADLAN (Associació d'Amis de L'Art Nou [Association of the Friends of New Art]) group and wrote for the magazine *D'Aci i D'Allá*. After the Civil War the tie remained strong and took shape in the creation of Club 49 and in his relationship with the *Dau al Set* group. In these years Prat moved his family hat business to the Rambla de Catalunya, and it became the meeting place for young artists and critics who had occasion to meet Miró there, as Portabella recounts, and other significant figures of Catalan culture. Prat's friendship with Miró lasted all his life, and the Miró Foundation in Barcelona holds a major donation from his personal collection.

2. Portabella is referring to important figures in Catalan culture from those years: the poet Joan Brossa (Barcelona, 1919–1998), who met Miró through Joan Prats in 1941 and who, from that point on, composed visual poems and poetic objects based on an interest in the irrational, Dadaism, and Surrealism. Together with the philosopher and critic Arnau Puig (Barcelona, 1926), Brossa founded the journal *Algol* and the following year the journal *Dau al Set*, where other painters, Antoni Tàpies (Barcelona, 1923–2012) among them, also participated. Arnau Puig was the theorist behind the *Dau al Set* group of artists that grew out of the journal and promoted, until 1951, an art closely tied to Surrealism in which these three were directly involved. This movement followed the resurgence of Surrealism in Paris, with the exhibit in 1947. In the mid fifties, when Portabella refers to his relationship with these three, the painter Antoni Tàpies, who had lived in Paris, had abandoned the fantastic figurative character of his painting tied to *Dau al Set*, in favor of a style based on the material and a personal language, through which he was beginning to be known and to receive major international recognition.

3. The May Day celebration was established in 1889 by the Second Socialist International to commemorate the Haymarket Riots that took place in Chicago in 1886. The celebration fosters the expression of working-class demands and is comparable, in a certain sense, to Labor Day in the United States. In 1968 May Day celebrations in Spain were marked by the Franco regime's repression. The Comisiones Obreras labor union, referred to in the interview, was among the groups who called for strikes and demonstrations, and one of the major players in the underground opposition to the regime. In general terms the 1968 disturbances in Spain were characterized by the lack of political freedom imposed by the regime and the desire to bring the mobilization of the working class together with cultural expression. Clearly its impact in Spain was more modest than in other European capitals, particularly Paris.

4. Carles Santos (Vinaroz, Castellón, 1940), a composer and pianist influenced by Fluxus, and the poet Joan Brossa were the authors of the *Concert Irregular* [Irregular Concert] that debuted on July 22, 1968, at the Maeght Foundation in Saint-Paul-de-Vence (France), on the occasion of an exhibit dedicated to Miró, and was staged in October of that year in the Teatre Romea in Barcelona, with the participation of the mezzo-soprano Anna Ricci. Pere Portabella was responsible for the mise-en-scène. In 1973 Carles Santos and Portabella were part of the experimental art group *Grup de Treball*, which brought together conceptual art and political activism.

5. The Eina School of Barcelona was founded in 1967 by the art critic Alexandre Cirici and the painter Albert Ràfols Casamada as a design school that sought to bring together design and art with an independent and avant-garde spirit. During the sixties it included the participation of experimental and conceptual artists in Catalonia. Today it is part of the University of Barcelona.

6. *Calçotadas* is a springtime festival in Catalonia where people eat roasted young green onions with romesco sauce.

7. The Barceloneta is the maritime neighborhood of Barcelona, built in the eighteenth century. It is the area of the city where in the nineteenth century the major factories were located, is related to port activities, and is also the district where the most important beach in Barcelona is located, which goes by the same name.

8. This is the name by which the court martial that took place in the city of Burgos from December 3 to 28, 1970, was known. A military jury tried a total of sixteen militants of the Basque opposition group ETA, among whom were two priests, and the trial ended with six death penalties that were finally commuted to life sentences. The court martial was seen as putting the anti-Franco opposition on trial, both in Spain and beyond its borders. In Catalonia the trial was the stimulus for a clandestine assembly in the Monastery of Montserrat that brought together intellectuals and artists, which Pere Portabella refers to and in which Miró and Tàpies, among others, took part.

9. Opus Dei is a Catholic organization founded in 1928 by José María Escrivá de Balaguer that spread throughout Europe and the rest of the world after World War II. In 1950 it was recognized by the Vatican as a Secular Institute and since 1982 is the Personal Prelature of the Catholic Church. The influence of the members of this organization on the Franco government grew throughout the fifties, and its ministers were considered "technocrats," holding important positions related primarily to industry, commerce, and foreign affairs, with an ideology defined as liberal capitalism, giving the Franco regime a more modern image.

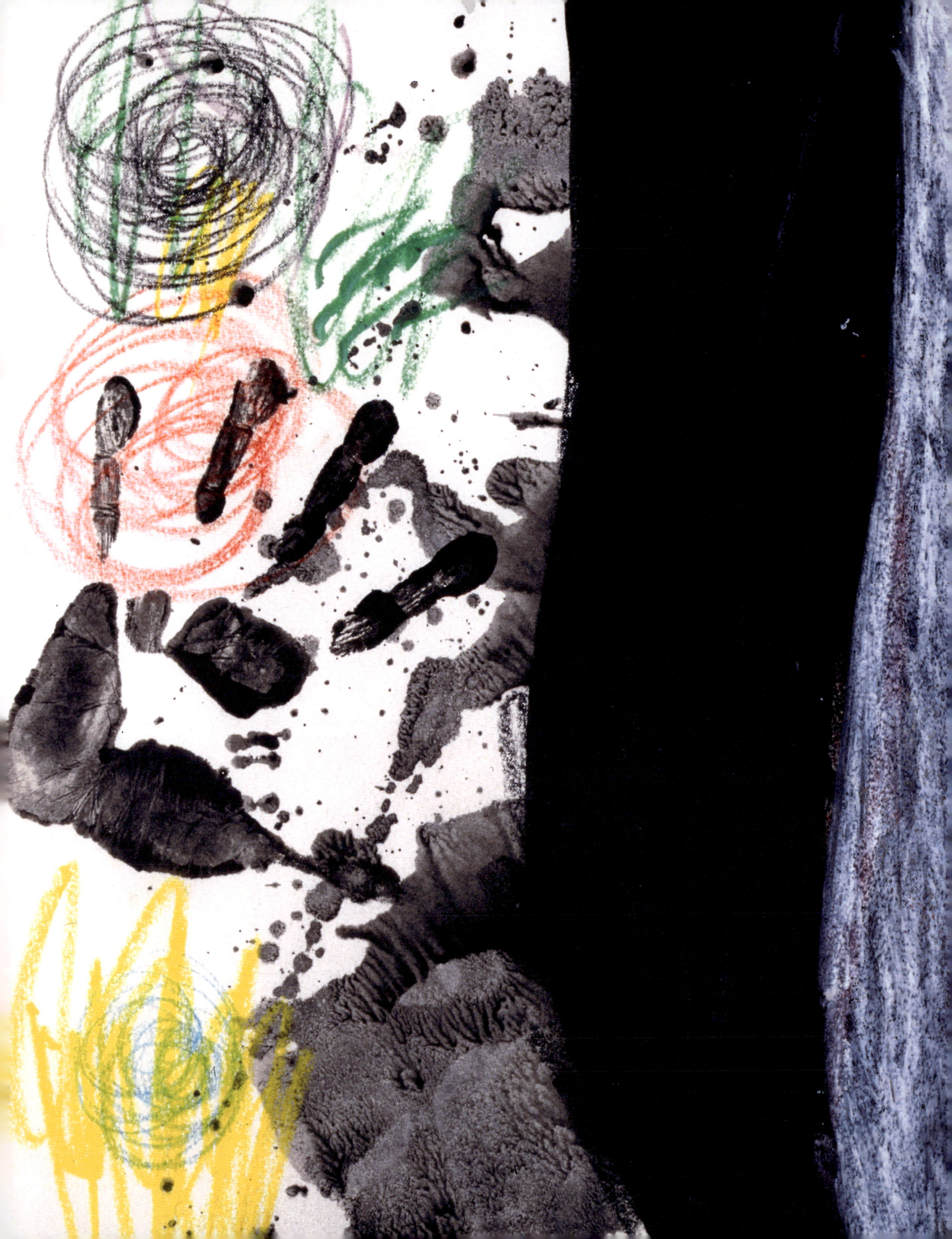

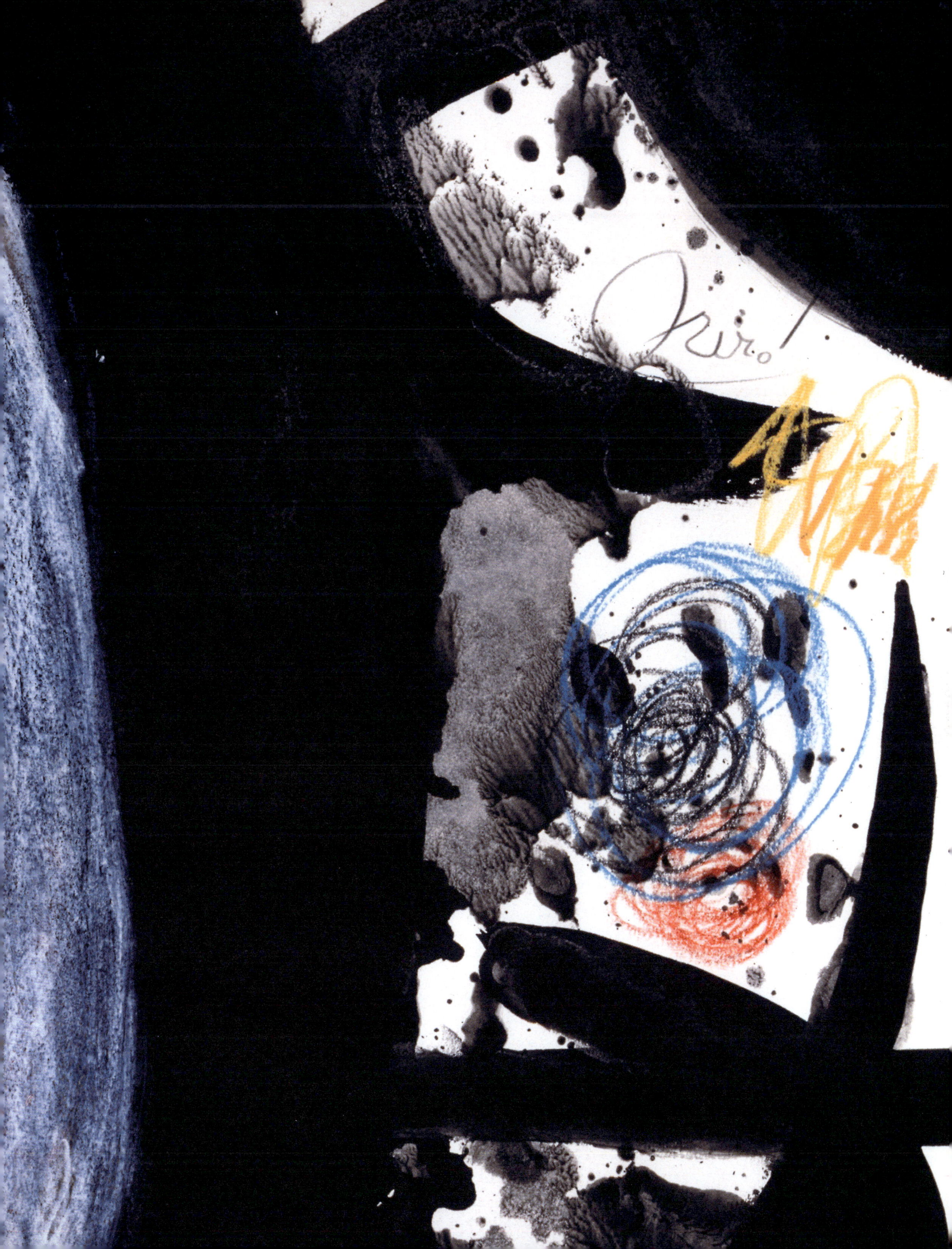
Miró

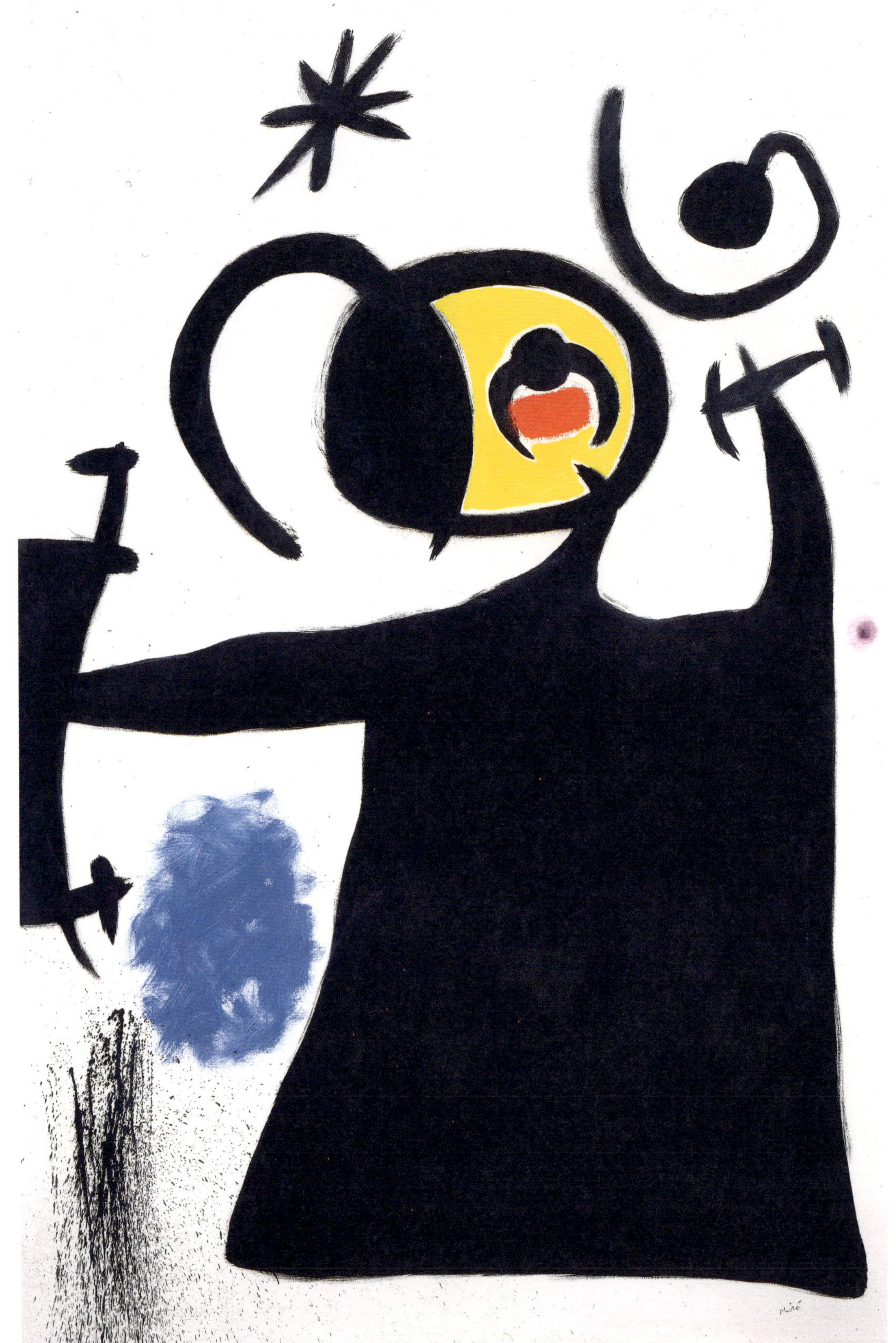

Femme en transe par la fuite des étoiles filantes (Woman Entranced by the Escape of Shooting Stars)
1969, acrylic on canvas, 76¾ × 51 3/16 in. (195 × 130 cm)

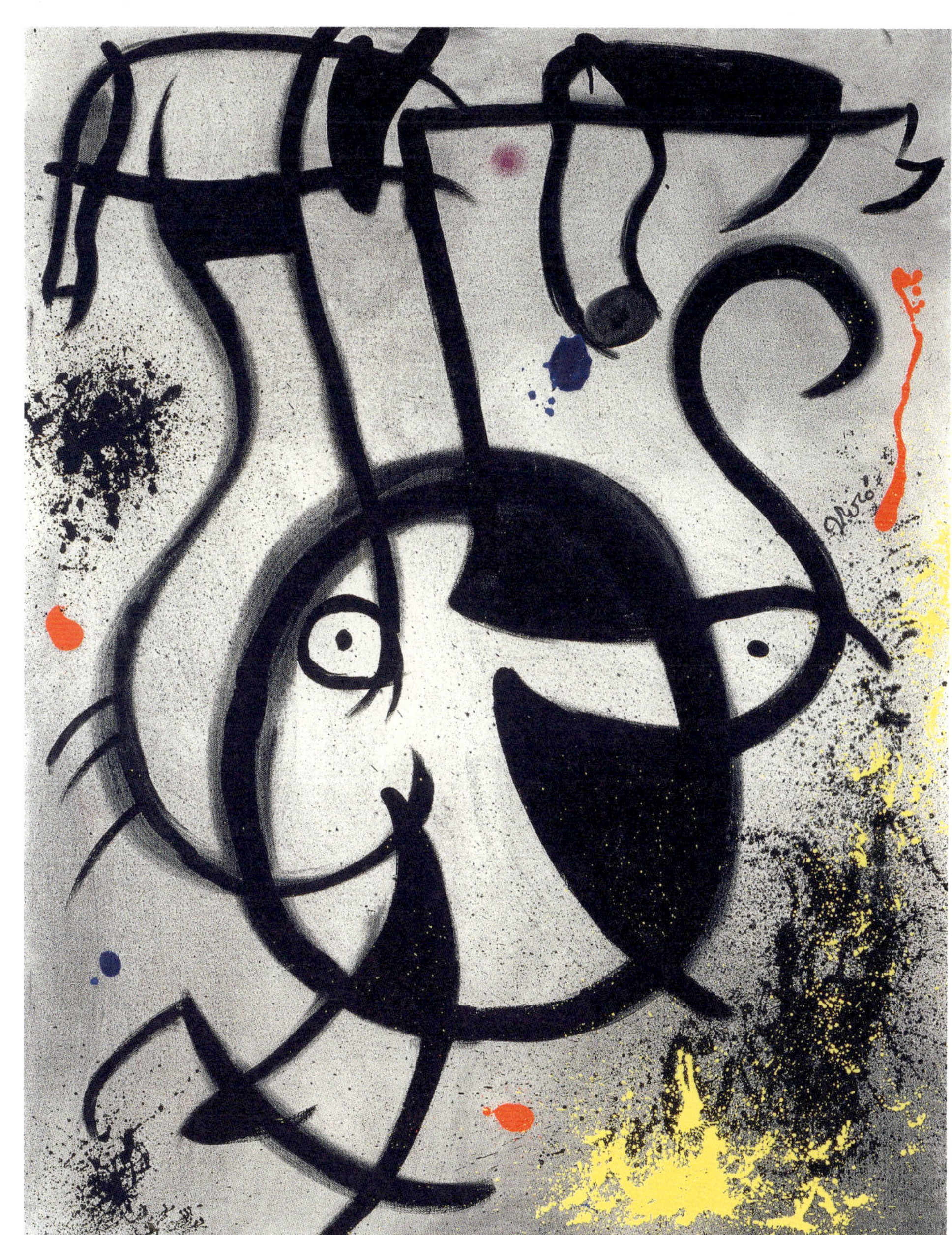

Femme espagnole (Spanish Woman), 1974, oil on canvas, 57½ × 44⅞ in. (146 × 114 cm)

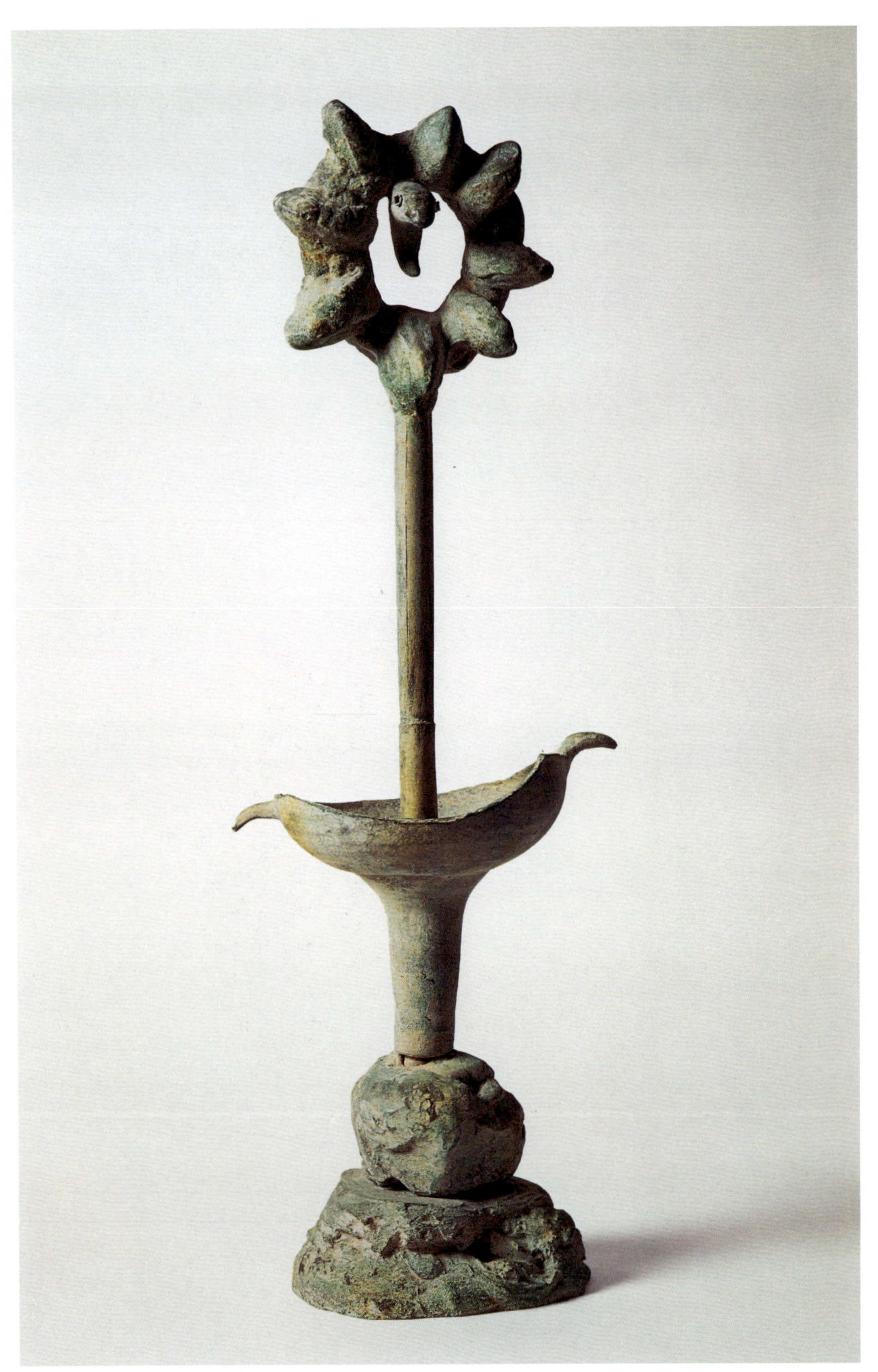

Femme au soleil (Sun Woman), 1966, patinated bronze, 33¹⁄₁₆ × 11 × 8⁷⁄₁₆ in. (84 × 28 × 21.5 cm)

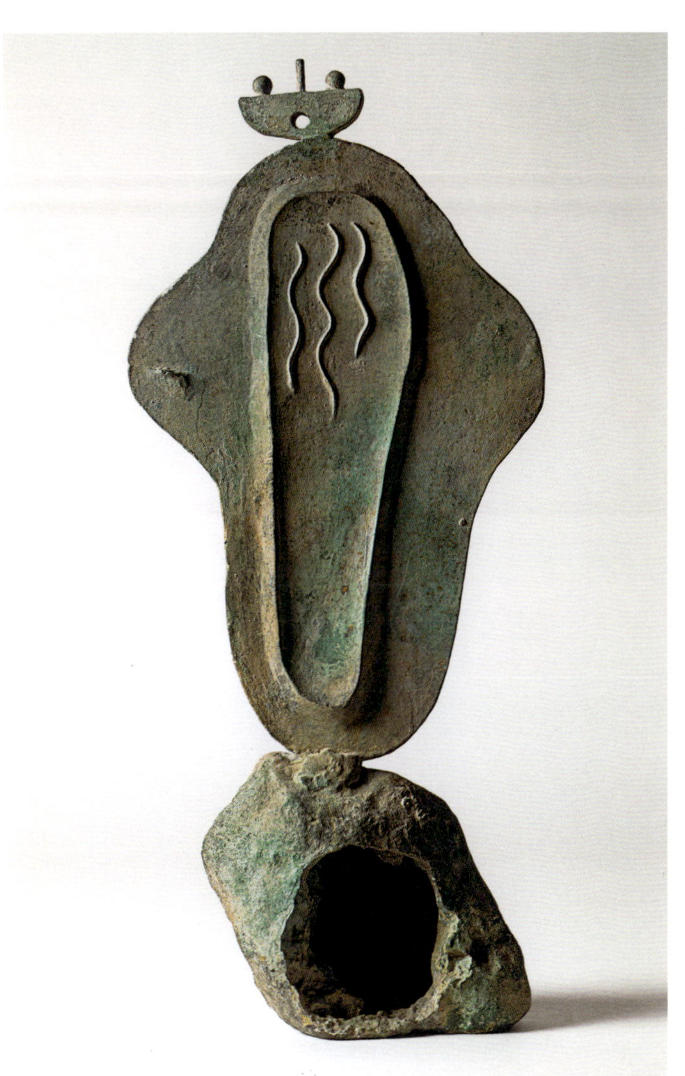

Femme dans la nuit (Woman in the Night), 1967, patinated bronze, 24 7/16 × 11 5/8 × 4 5/16 in. (62 × 29.5 × 11 cm), front. Back view below.

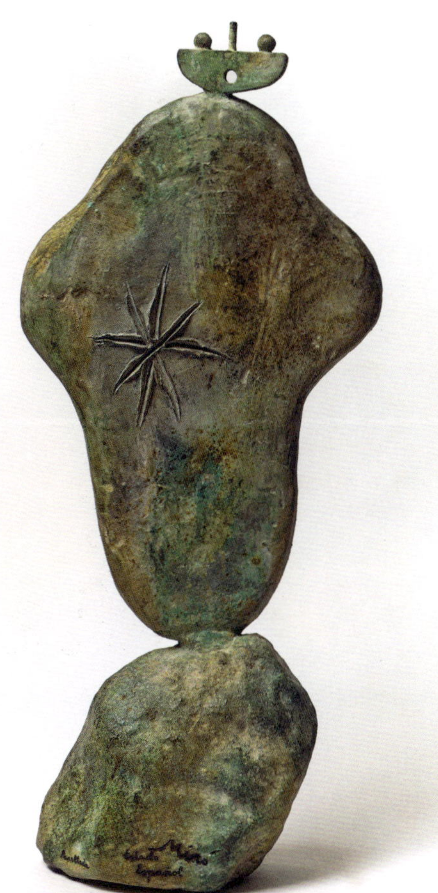

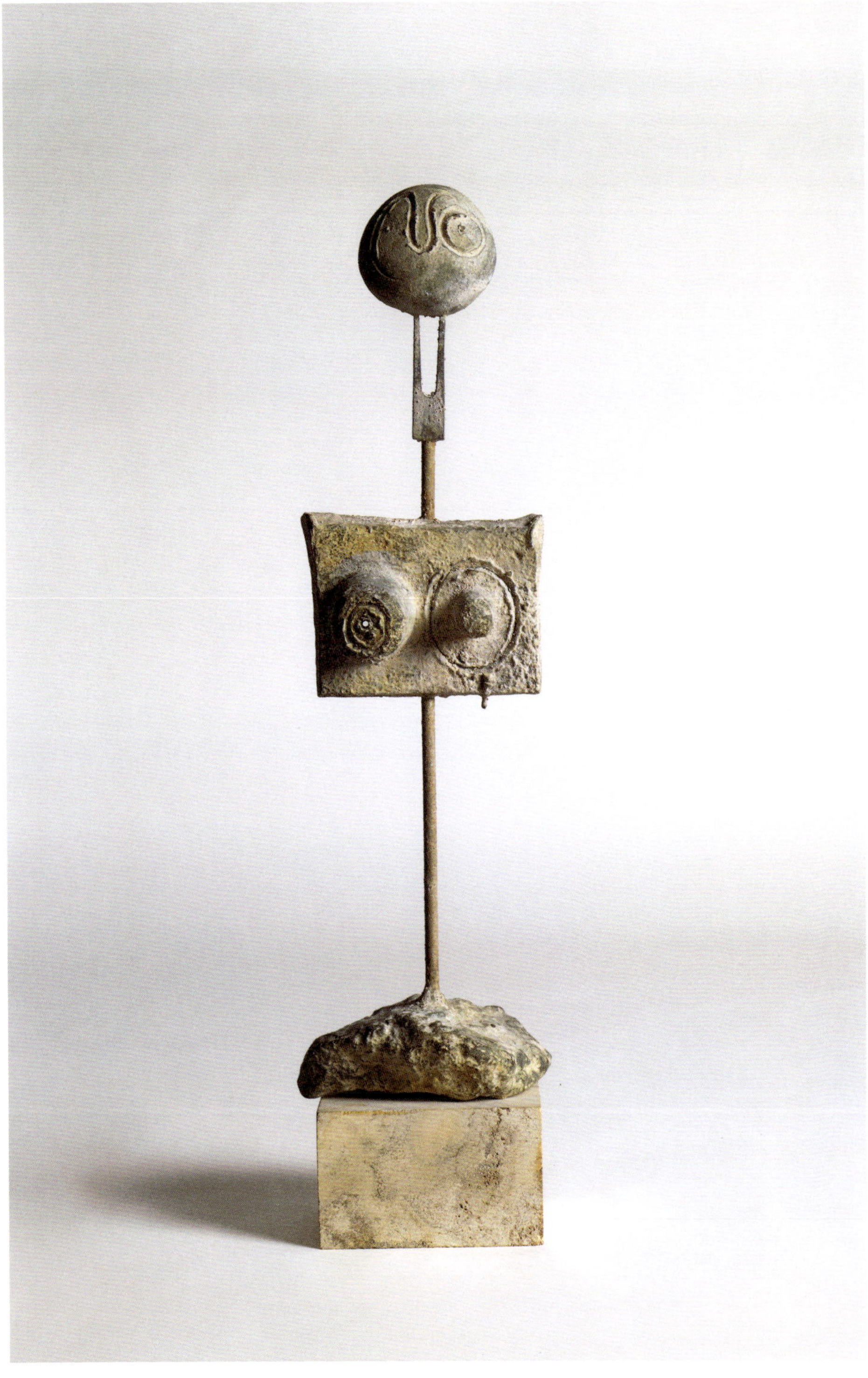

Femme aux beaux seins (Woman with Beautiful Breasts), 1969, patinated bronze, $18\frac{1}{2} \times 5\frac{1}{8} \times 3\frac{15}{16}$ in. (47 × 13 × 10 cm)

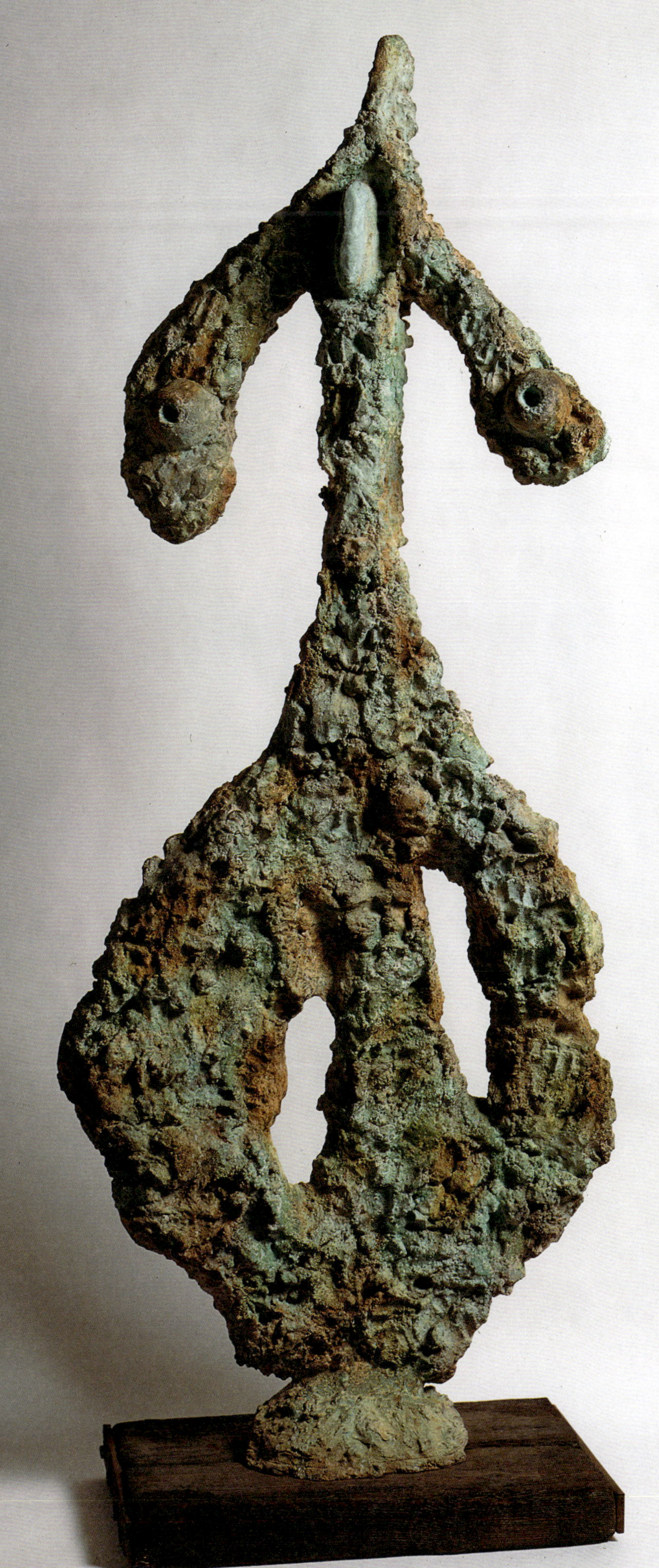

Femme (Woman), 1968, patinated bronze, 70 1/16 × 28 9/16 × 13 3/8 in. (178 × 72.5 × 34 cm)

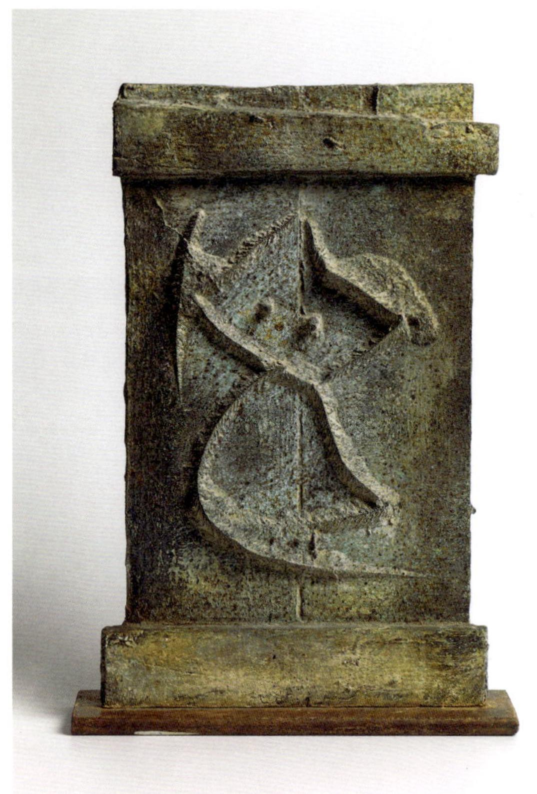

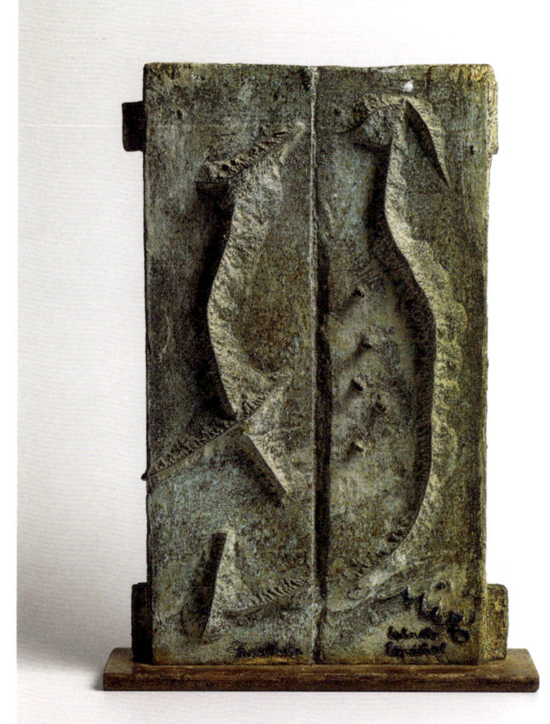

Bas-relief (Low Relief), 1969, patinated bronze, 14 × 8⅞ × 2¾ in. (35.5 × 22.5 × 7 cm), back. Front view above.

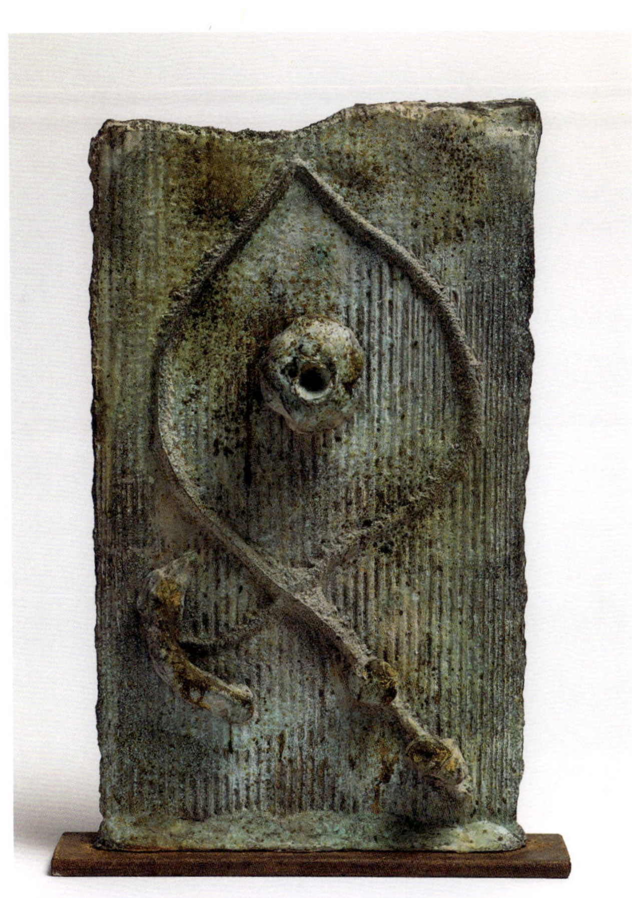

Bas-relief (Low Relief), 1970, patinated bronze, 17 5/16 × 11 13/16 × 4 5/16 in. (44 × 30 × 11 cm), front.
Back view below.

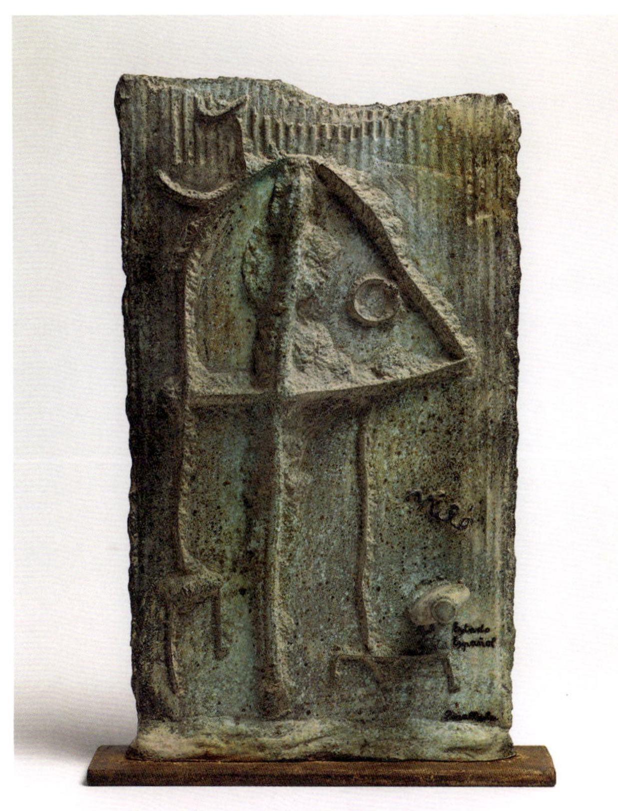

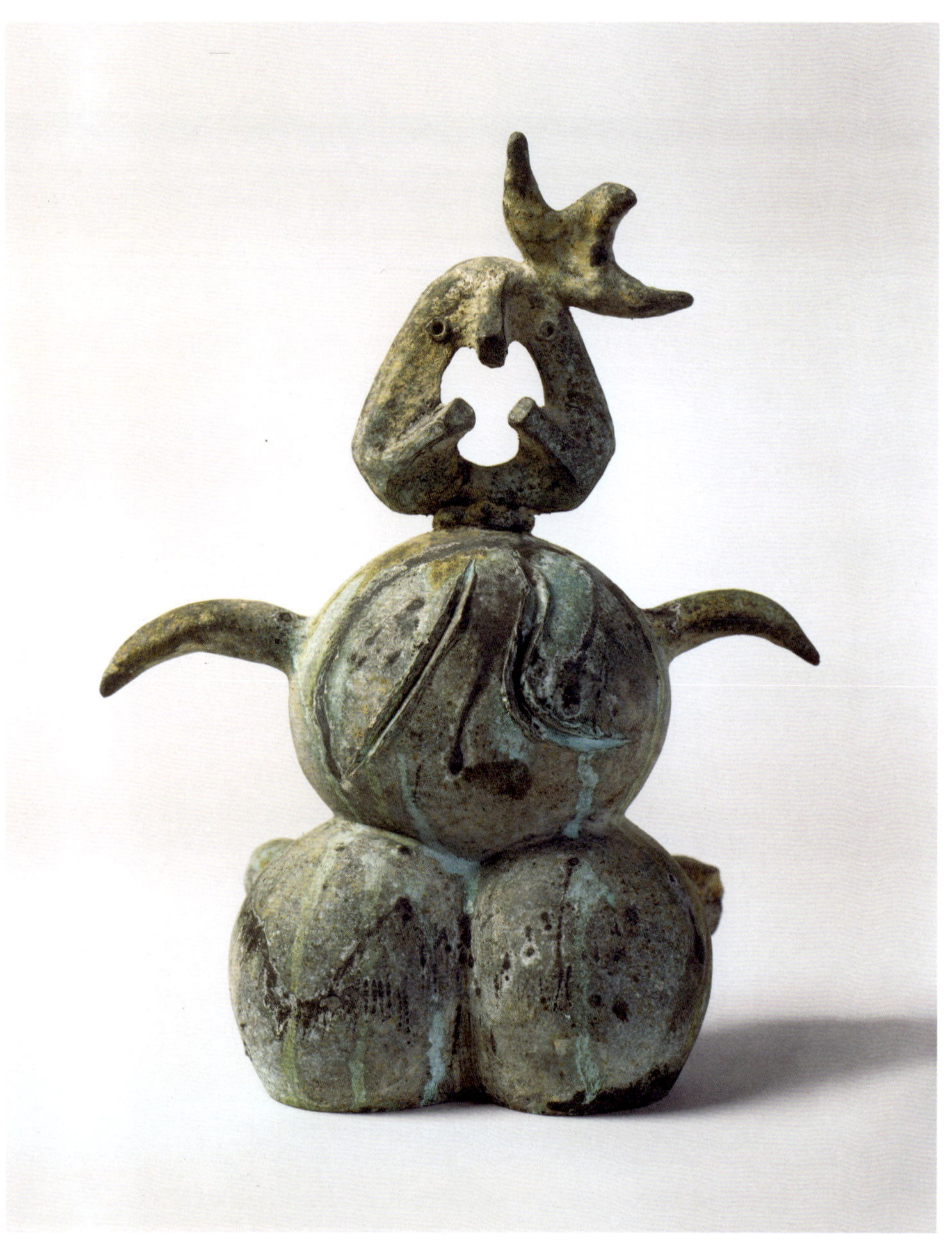

Femme et oiseau (Woman and Bird), 1968, patinated bronze, 12½ × 9¹³⁄₁₆ × 5⅞ in. (31.7 × 24.9 × 15 cm)

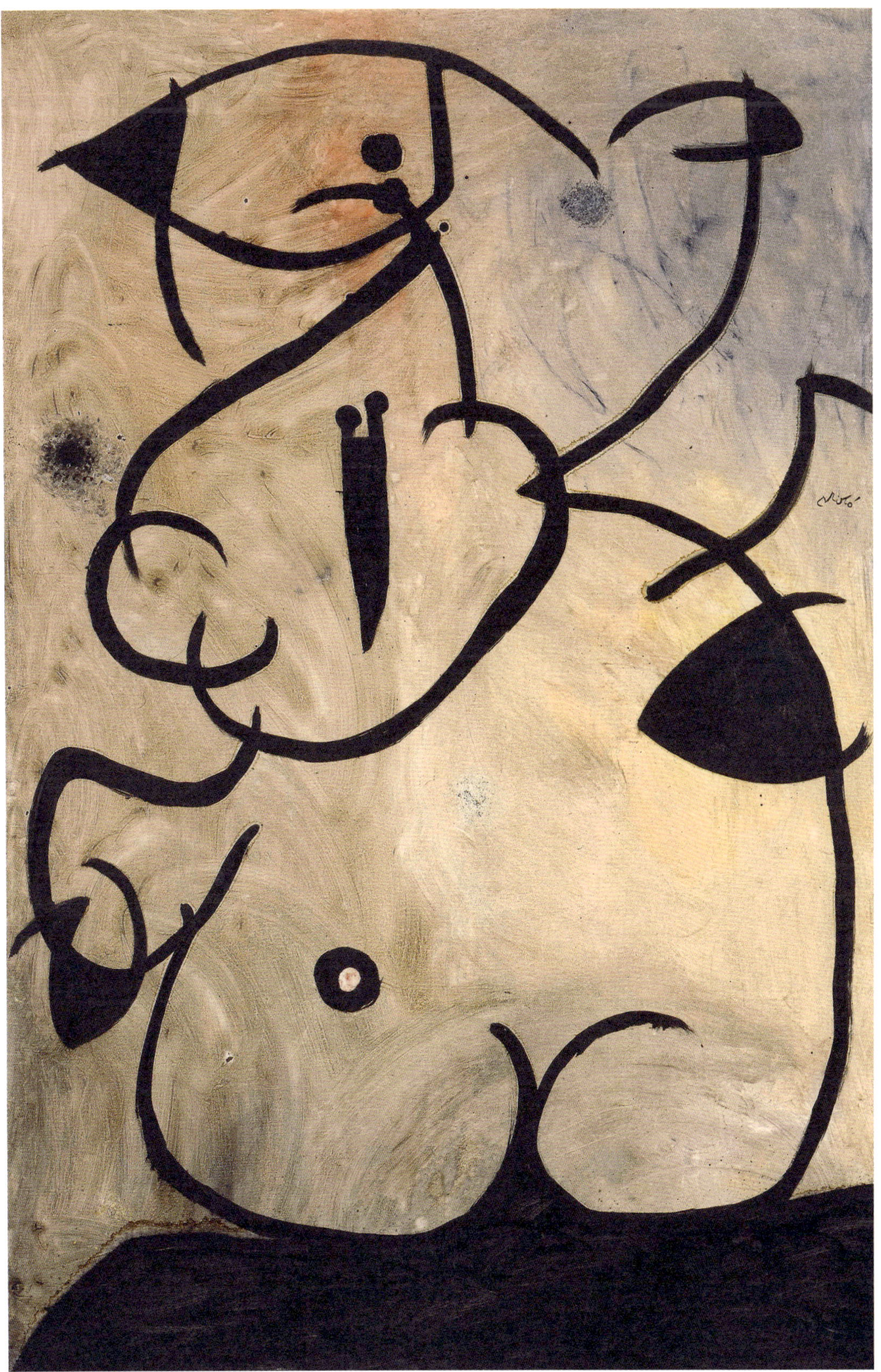

Femme oiseau II (Bird Woman II), 1977, oil on canvas, 76¾ × 51³⁄₁₆ in. (195 × 130 cm)

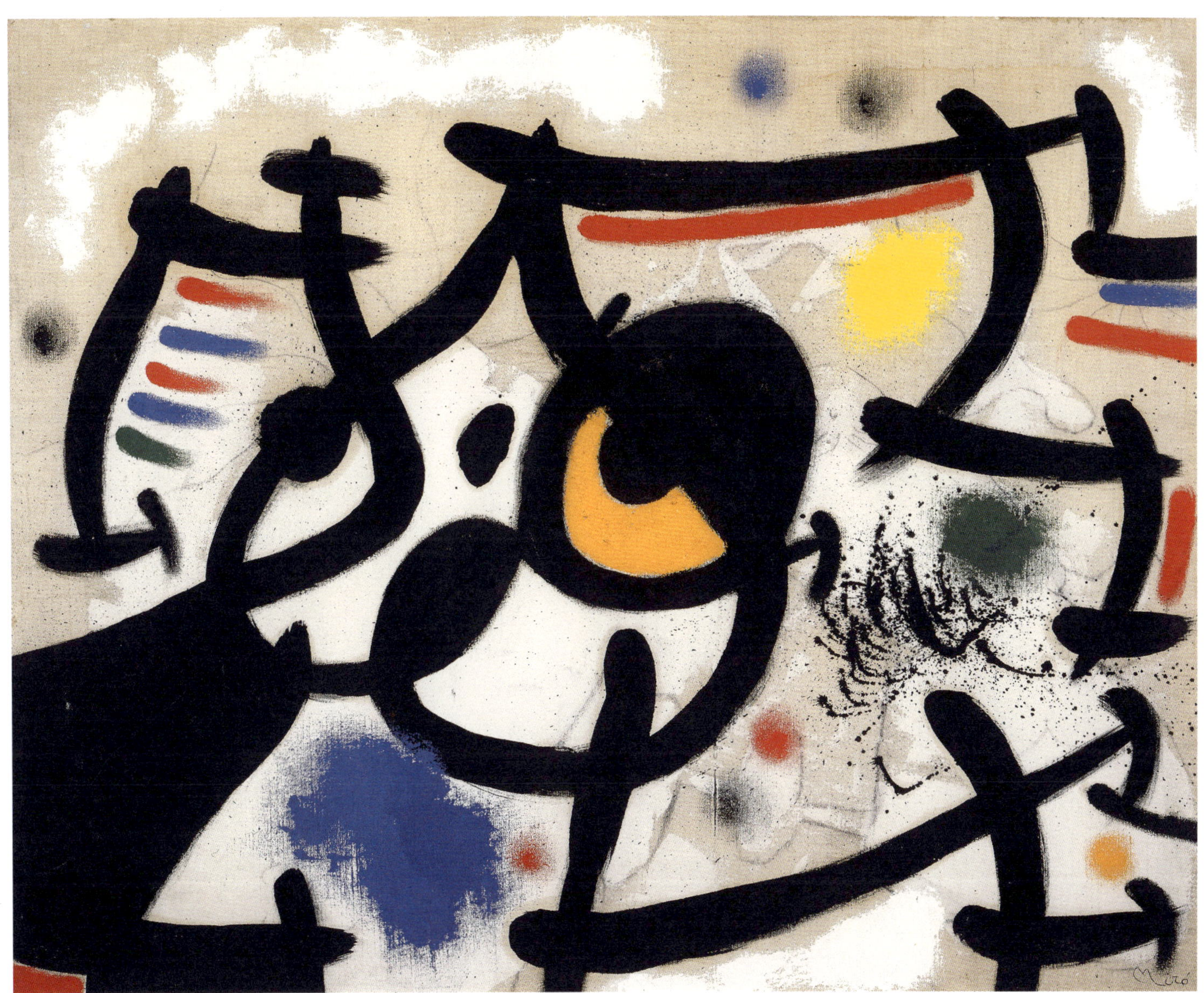

Femmes VI (Women VI), 1969, oil on canvas, 28¾ × 36¼ in. (73 × 92 cm)

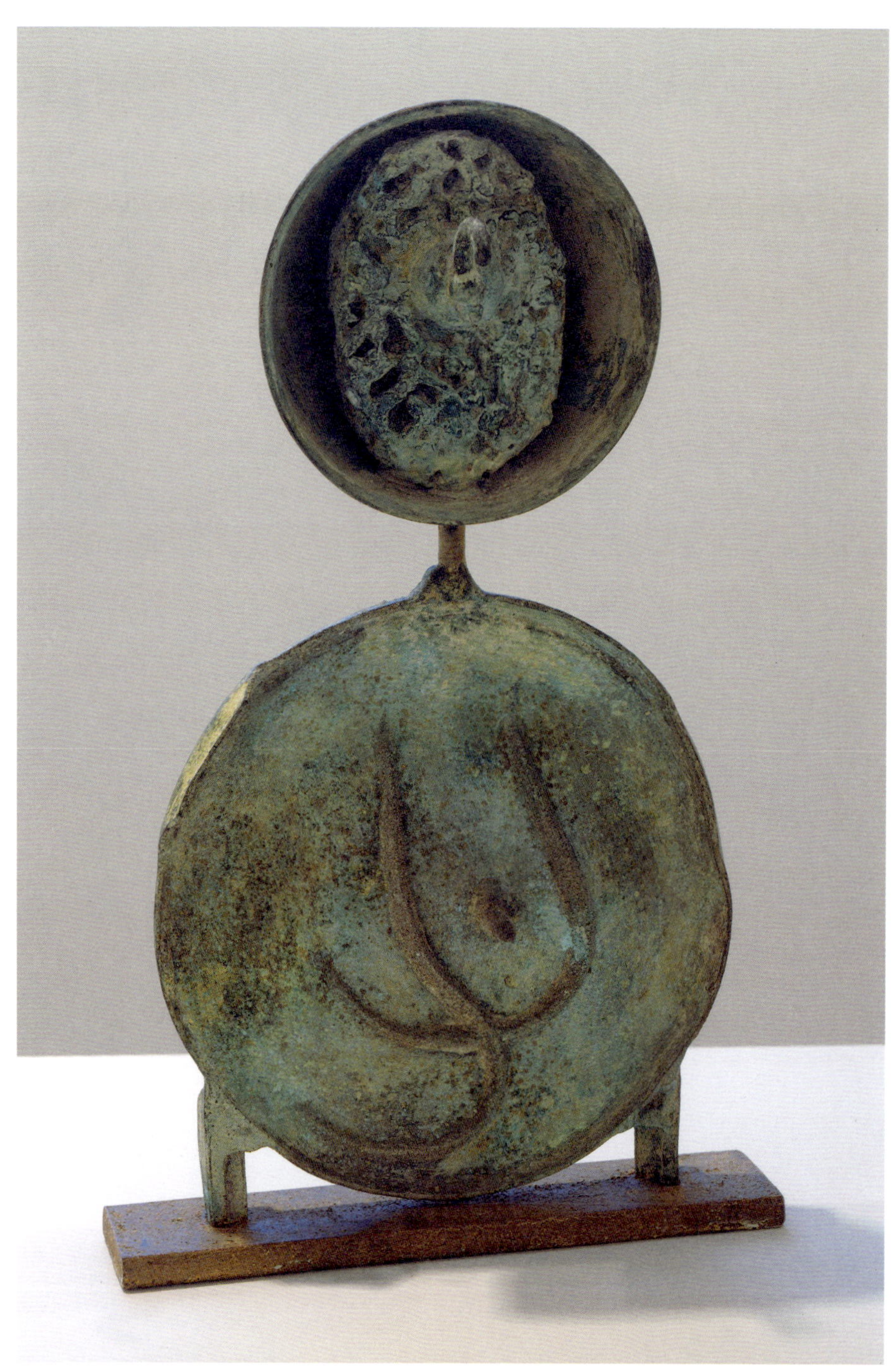

Jeune femme (Young Woman), 1973, patinated bronze, 14 3/16 × 8 11/16 × 3 9/16 in. (36 × 22 × 9 cm)

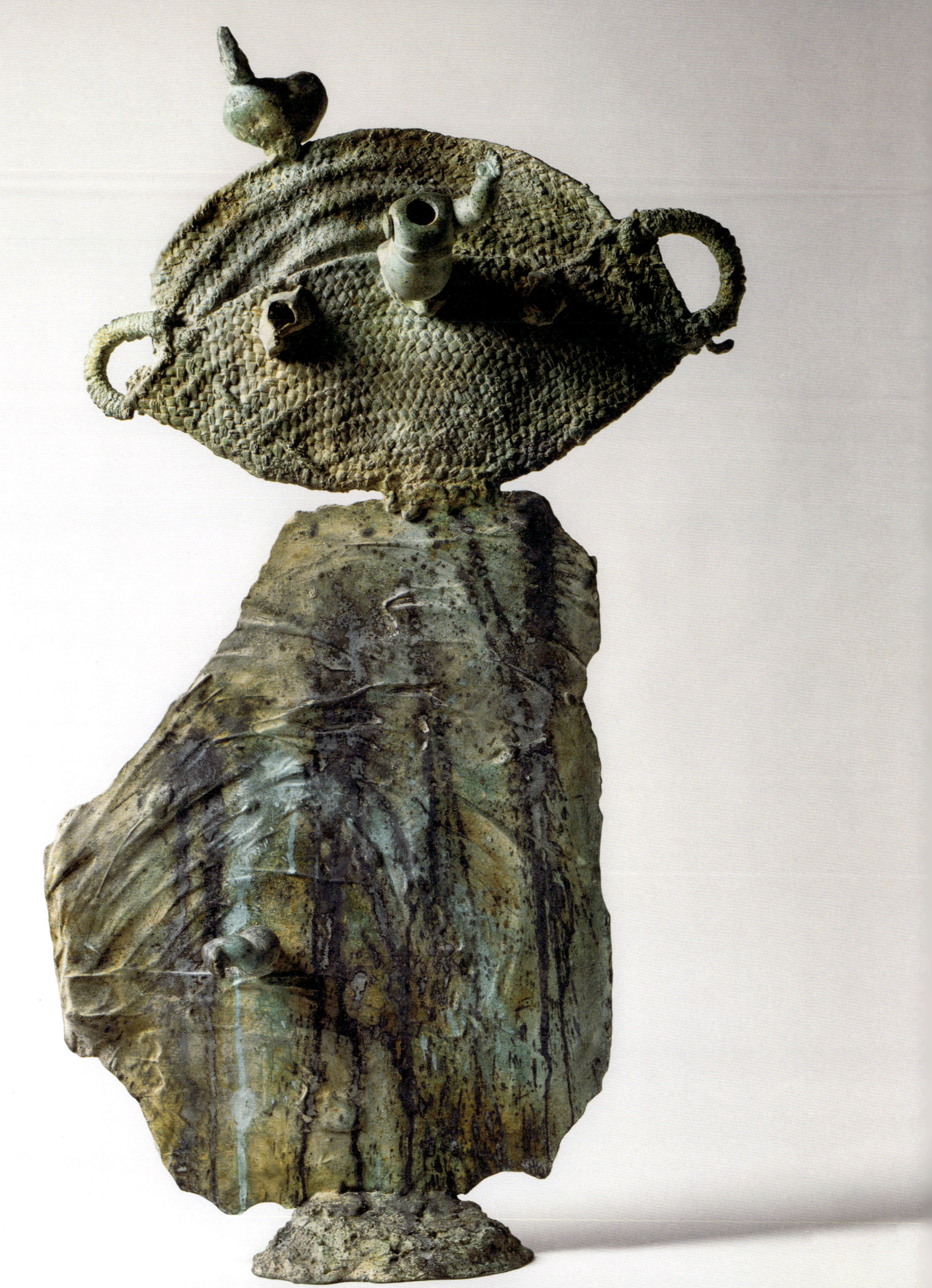

Personnage et oiseau (Figure and Bird), 1968, patinated bronze, 40 9/16 × 23 5/8 × 8 7/16 in. (103 × 60 × 21.5 cm). Detail on following page.

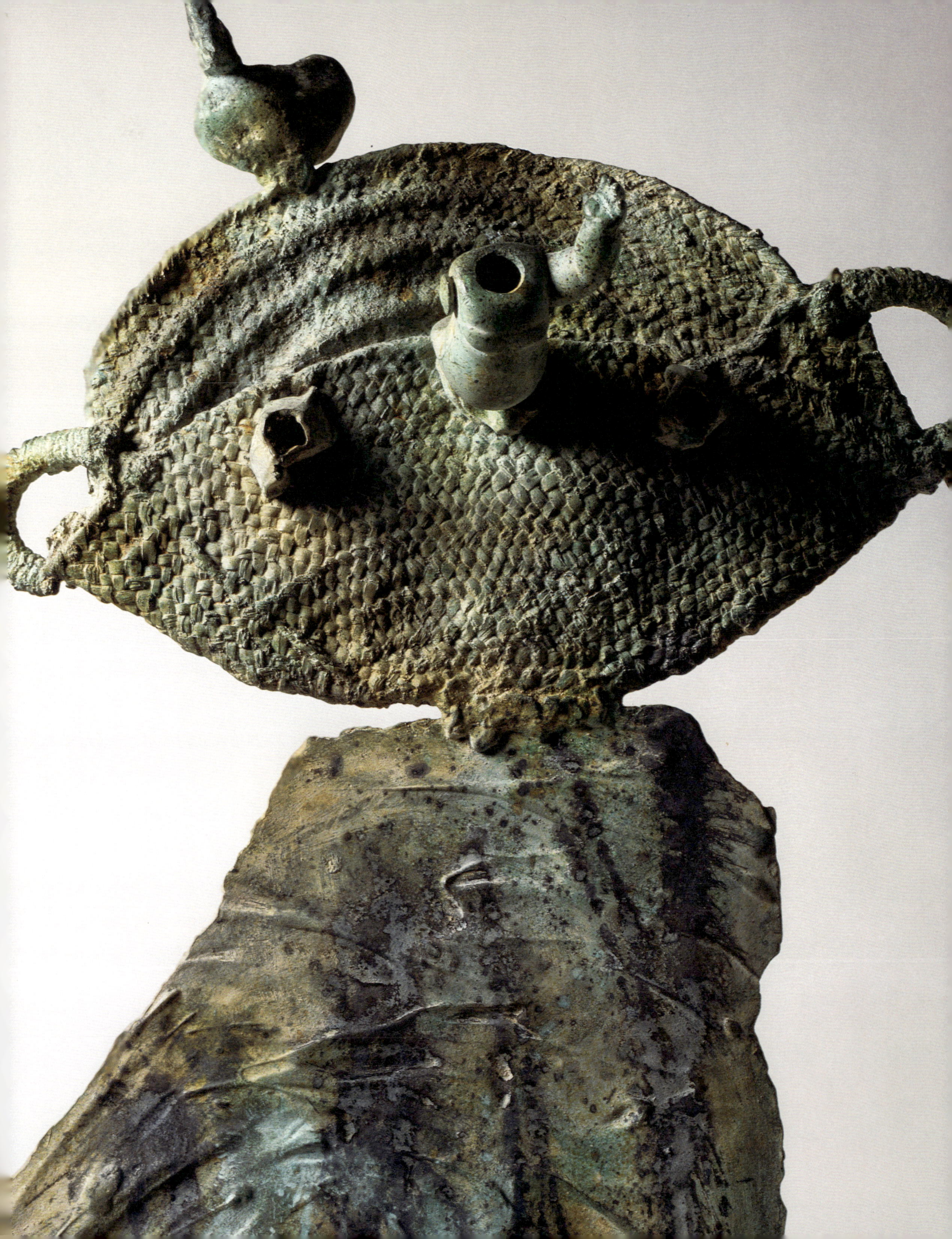

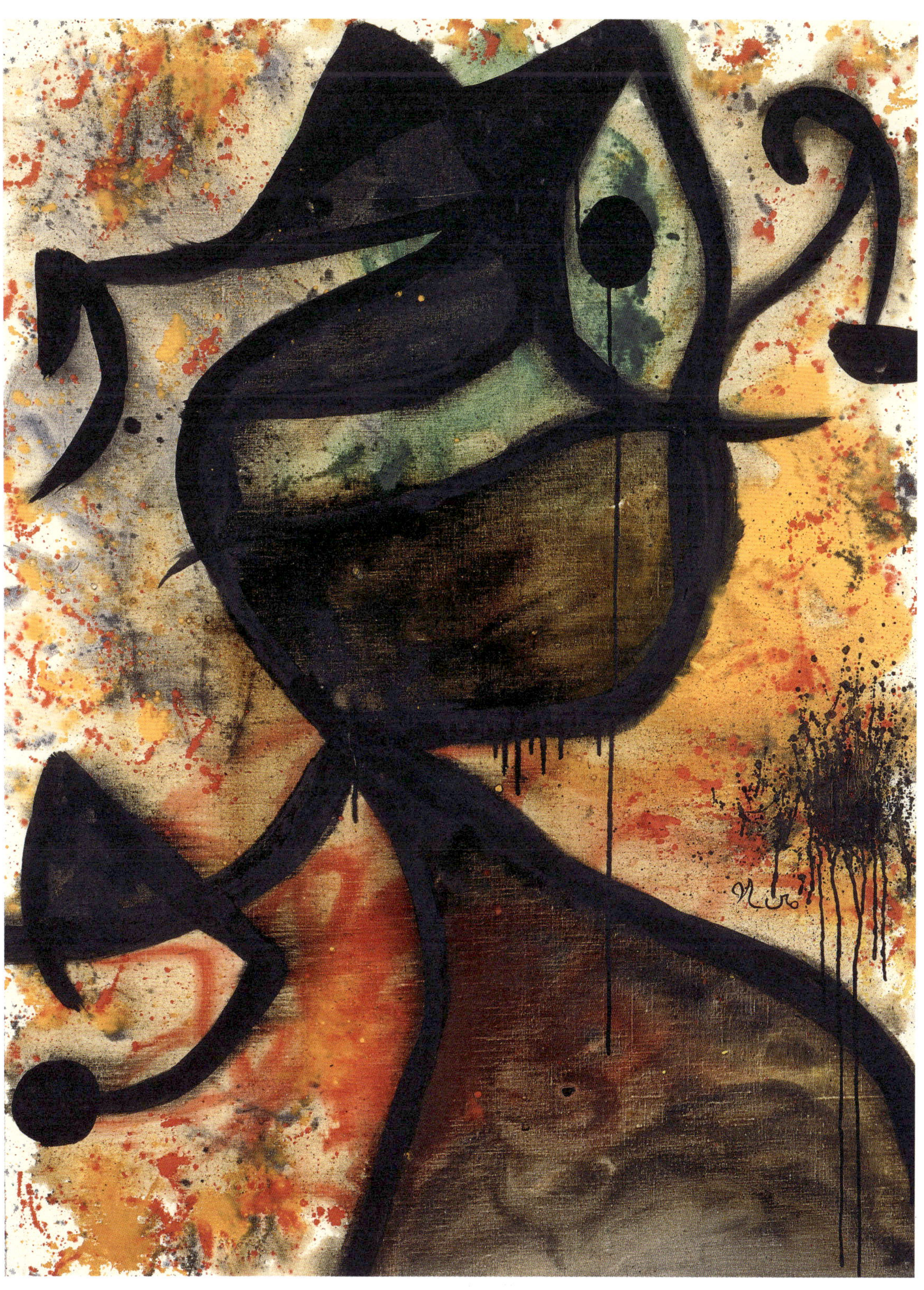

Personnage, oiseaux (Figure, Birds), 1974, oil on canvas, 45¹¹⁄₁₆ × 34⅝ in. (116 × 88 cm)

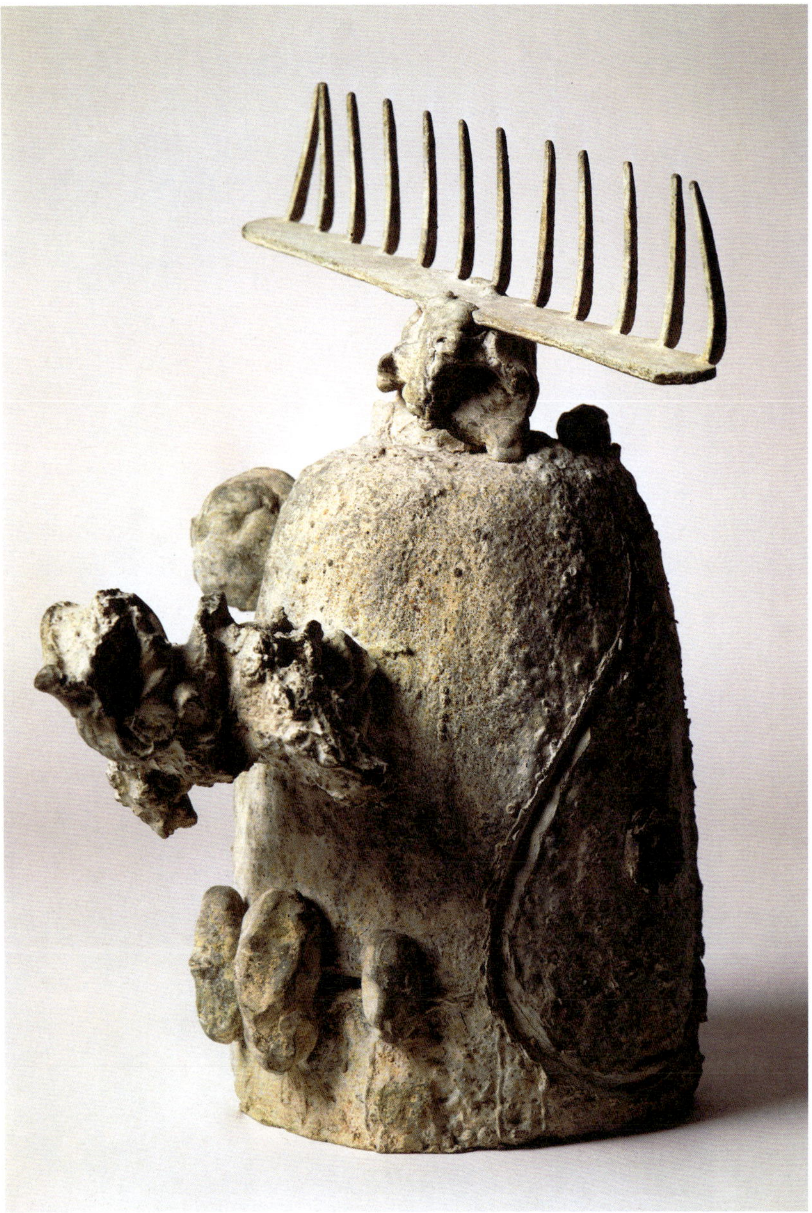

Tête et oiseau (Head and Bird), 1973, patinated bronze, 16⁹⁄₁₆ × 13 × 13⅜ in. (42 × 33 × 34 cm)

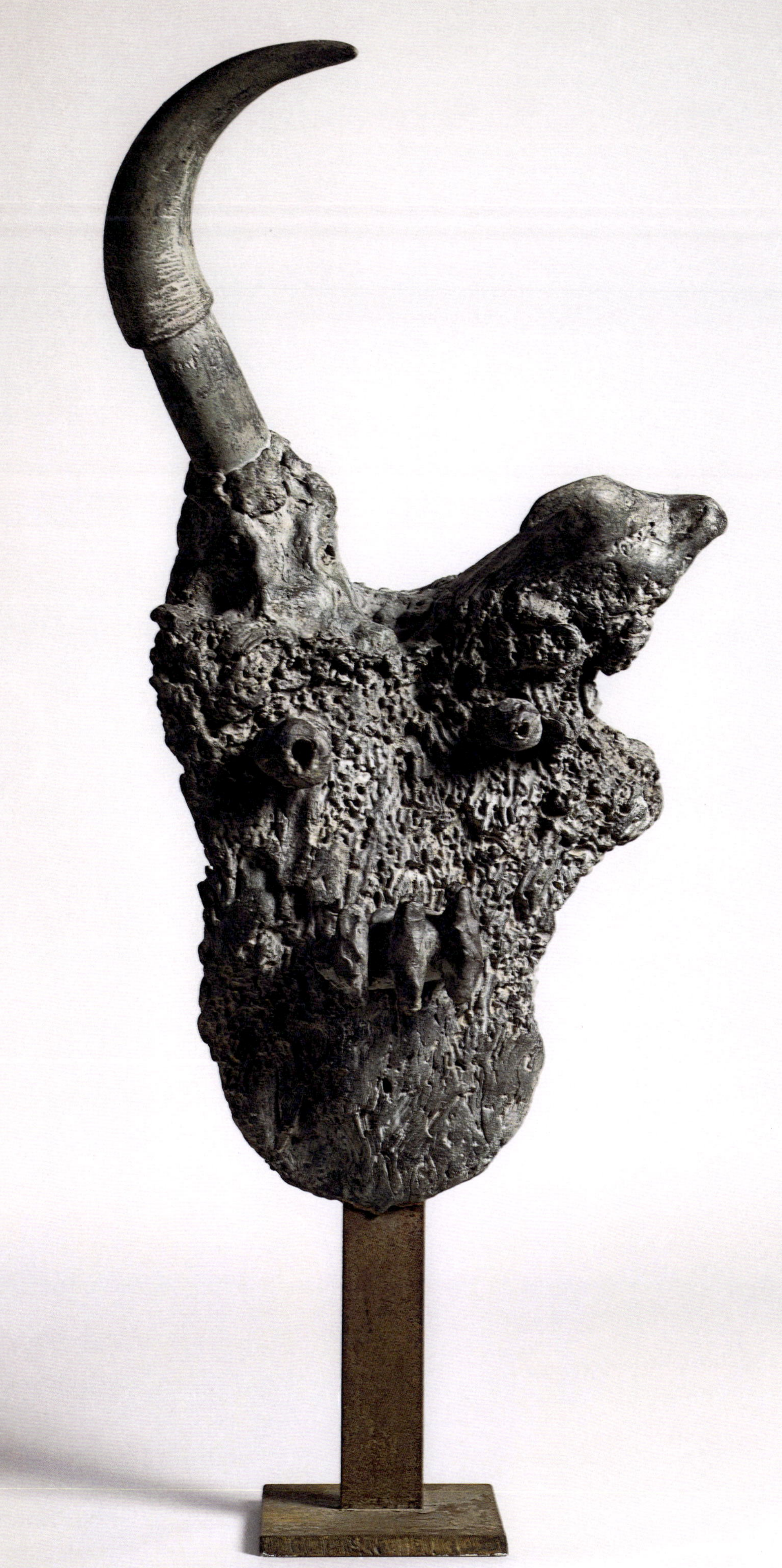

Tête de taureau (*Bull's Head*), 1970, patinated bronze, 39⅜ × 17 5/16 × 13 in. (100 × 44 × 33 cm)

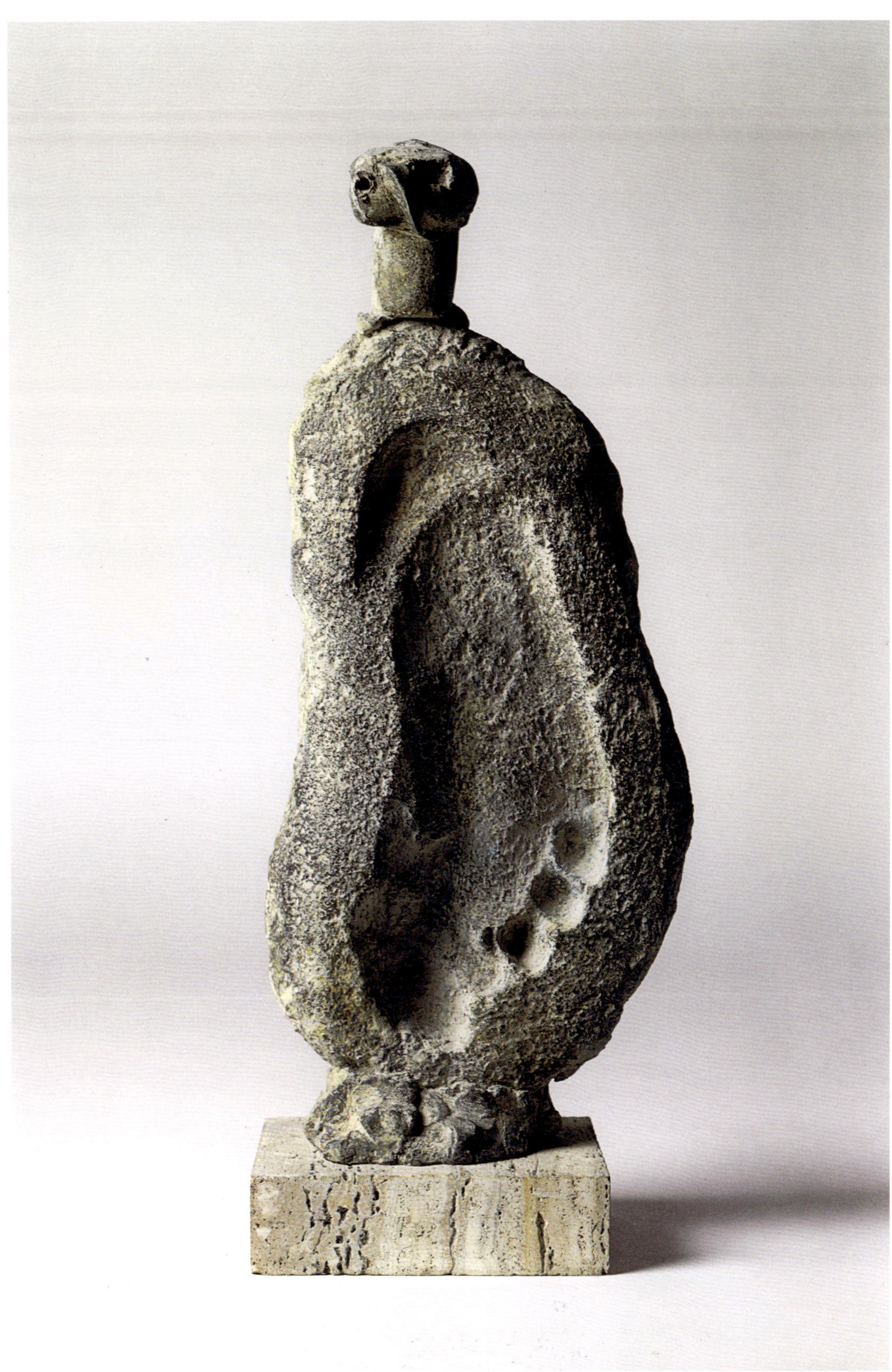

Figure, 1968, patinated bronze, 18 11/16 × 7 11/16 × 5 1/8 in. (47.5 × 19.5 × 13 cm)

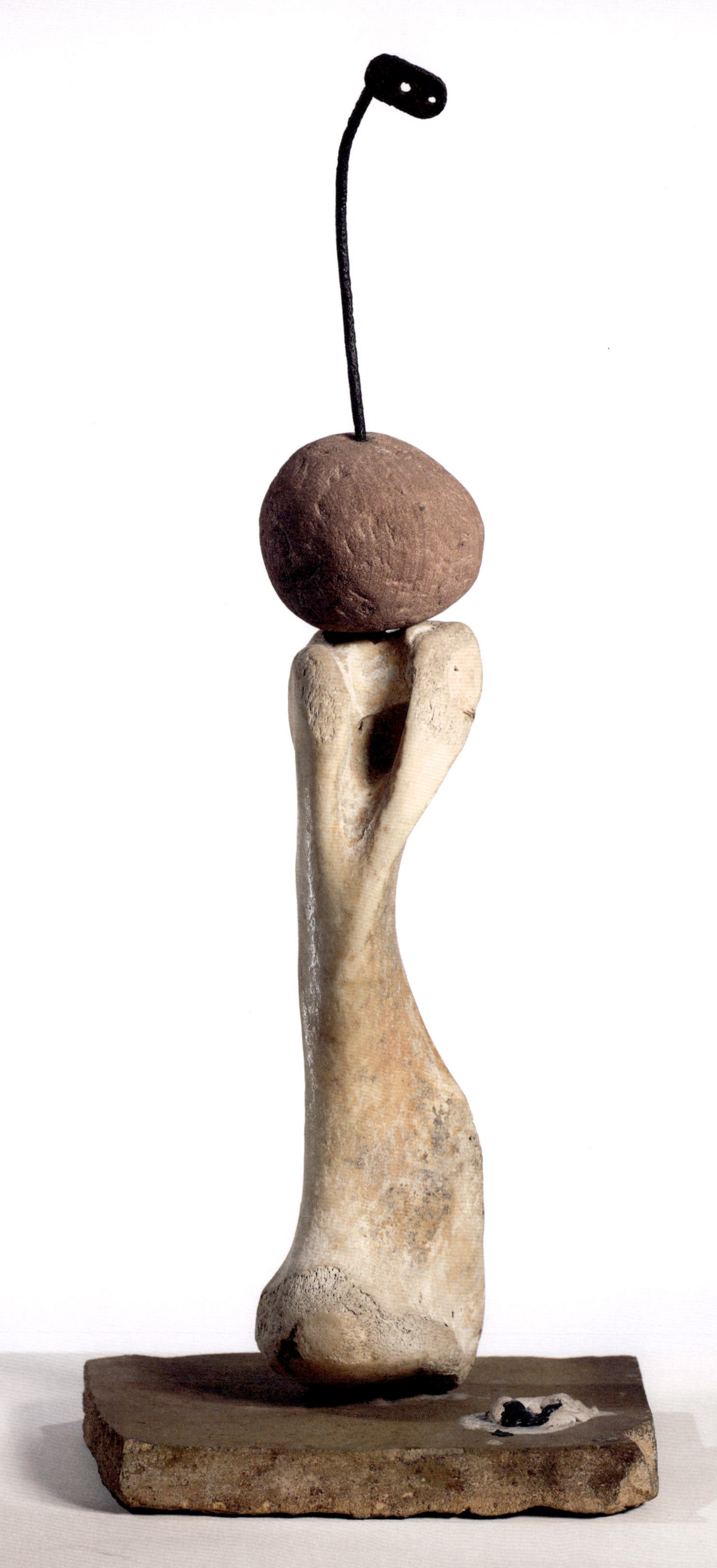

Femme (Woman)
1946
Bone, grindstone, iron, and oil on potter's clay
21¼ × 9 × 7½ in.
(54 × 23 × 19 cm)
Fundació Joan Miró, Barcelona

Joan Miró: "Forms give birth to other forms, constantly changing into something else"

Carmen Fernández Aparicio

It is not the work that counts, but the spirit's trajectory over the course of a life.*

I.

In the early 1940s, immersed in the climate of isolation and solitude provoked by the war in Europe, Joan Miró set out to begin slow, deliberate work, hoping that it would result in a fluid expression of emotion. In his notebook, he wrote: "I will make my work *emerge* naturally, like the song of a bird or the music of Mozart, with no apparent effort, but thought out at length and worked out from within."[1] During the twenties a similar analytical process, based on preliminary sketches in which he defined his visual signs and a spatial order, had accomplished the emancipation of his painting. This process had attracted resounding reviews by critics such as the independent Waldemar George, who considered him to be "a magnetizing character who slips through the cracks of analysis, who steps outside the box and displaces modern art's center of gravity," opening up "the infernal circle of modern painting."[2]

The Second World War brought about a shift in the historical and life cycles that shaped the trajectory of the painter who would come to have a leading role in the Parisian post-Dada avant-garde movement. Despite the bitter outcome of the Spanish Civil War, Miró decided to return to Spain. He moved to Palma de Mallorca and returned to Mont-roig, Catalonia, where previous artistic discoveries had taken place.[3] He began this new phase by planning out the various fields in which he wished to develop his work. Part of this plan was a desire to "manipulate life to be independent in painting, as true poets do."[4] At the end of that decade, his goal was to focus his attention on an active revisionary process of what he called "the work of a lifetime,"[5] as an experience of looking critically at his historical contribution. This process explicitly led him to conclude that the idea of the individual artist is less important than the creative act itself. The definitive codification of the work featured in this exhibition, which began in the sixties, is like a structure combined in two and three dimensions. It reflected a world in which, in Miró's own words, "everything becomes strange, shifting, clear and confused at the same time." He added that in this world: "Forms give birth to other forms, constantly changing into something else. They become each other and in this way create the reality of a universe of signs and symbols in which figures pass from one realm to another, their feet touching the roots, becoming roots themselves as they disappear into the flowing hair of the constellations."[6]

II.

The complex development of Miró's work from 1920, when he took his first trip to Paris, to the completion of *Constellations* (January 1940 to September 1941), was a determining factor in the later evolution of the works he would produce at the height of his career. *Constellations* was a set of twenty-three gouaches that made up the temporal core of Miró's contribution to the historical avant-garde—his "work of a lifetime." This development process carried Miró away from the level of detail in *The Farm* (1921–22), where each element of the landscape is represented meticulously in a frontal spatial structure derived from Synthetic Cubism, and toward pictorial illusionism. This concept can be seen especially in *The Tilled Field* (1923–24) and *The Hunter (Catalan Landscape)* (1923–24; p. 43, bottom). In these works, the objects and metonymic signs are dispersed over a background of color fields.[7] The so-called Oneiric Paintings[8] were influenced

*Joan Miró, "Un femme," in *Joan Miró: Los cuadernos catalanes,* ed. Gaëtan Picon (Barcelona: Polígrafa, 1980): 128.

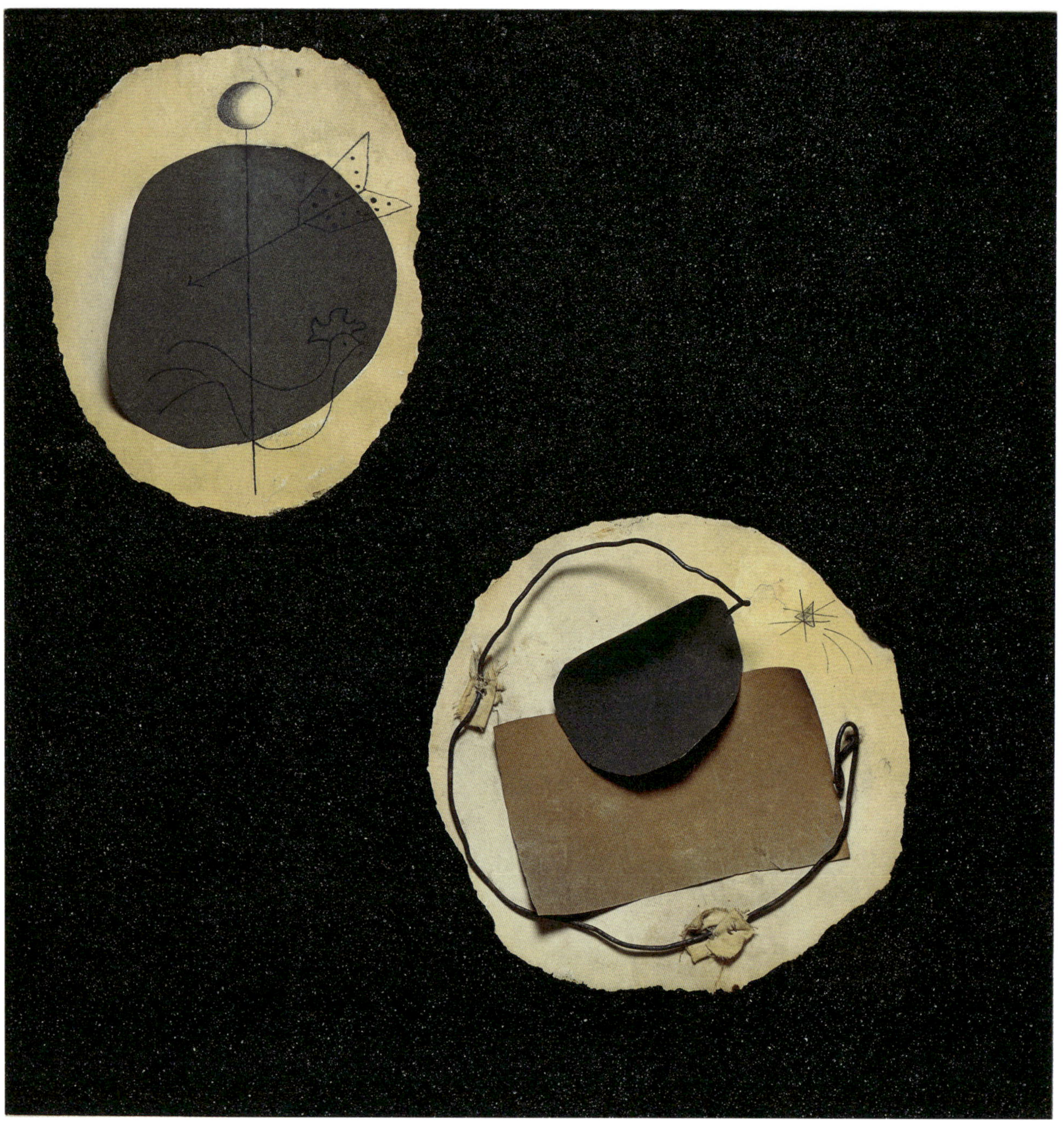

Collage
Mont-roig, 1929
Asphalt plaque, various papers cut and pasted, wire, rags, ink, and crayon
29⁵⁄₁₆ × 29 × 2¾ in.
(74.4 × 73.7 × 7 cm)
Musée National d'Art Moderne, Centre Georges Pompidou, Paris, France

by the poetic practices of the Surrealist group at 45 Rue Blomet.[9] Their influence led Miró to paint monochromatic canvases that were structured like visual poems and sprinkled with signs dissociated from reality, in keeping with Surrealist automatism.[10] In 1933, following that interpretation that ignored the conscious actions of the artist, Joan Miró declared in an interview with the Surrealist magazine *Minotaure*: "It is difficult for me to talk about my painting, since it is always born in a state of hallucination, brought on by some jolt or other—whether objective or subjective—which I am not in the least responsible for."[11] He insisted on an interpretation that Maurice Raynal had recognized in 1927, citing his intention to "assassiner la peinture" (assassinate painting), and declaring him "le chef de L'École surréaliste."[12] Later, in 1928,[13] André Breton, the leader of the Surrealists, would write that he had become "the most surrealist of us all."[14] Despite his initial enthusiastic reception of Miró's work, Breton later grew suspicious of Miró's essential artistic sense. Miró had affinity for the spiritual capacity of Paul Klee's painting and an interest in the "formal beauty" of painting,[15] which Breton did not share.[16] As the Surrealist writer Michel Leiris remembered, this sort of beauty was characteristic of the Rue Blomet group's literary practices.[17] In late 1924 and early 1925 the members of this group, who aligned themselves with Breton's

Surrealism, sought a shift in which automatism and contrasts of irrationality began to fade out in favor of "a coherence comparable to that of a live organism or a musical structure."[18] This explained why Miró's preparatory works were more closely related to those subjective states that the painter called "hallucinatory"[19] than his paintings, which were full of compositional rigor.

Owing to his free and independent spirit and his aversion to dogmatism, during those years Joan Miró's relationship with the official Surrealist movement (to which he was never an adherent) was interestingly ambiguous. The poet Robert Desnos, his other close friend from the Rue Blomet, explained this relationship on the occasion of a 1929 Surrealist exhibition in Zurich, writing that "Miró's painting is without a doubt the purest in the world, in the same way that the painter is one of the purest spirits of our times."[20] With the new decade, the disagreements by Leiris and Bataille with respect to Breton's positions, as well as the birth of abstract groups, made their critical reception evolve.[21] From this point on, the reception of Miró's work goes beyond a strict correlation between the official Surrealism and so-called automatism at the same time that their paintings showed a radical change inspired by the primitive states of man.[22] A great deal of Miró's work in these years of social and anti-pictorial crisis attached itself to the technique of collage, which the Surrealists had revisited because it was a position radically opposed to painting. For Miró, as the writer Louis Aragon perceived, collage was characterized in terms of a radical and constant attraction to the materials he associated with his painting.[23]

Besides the abstract collages of 1929, tridimensionality emerged for Miró from the tarred, bored, or detached edges of pieces of sandpaper, as well as fabric and wire (opposite page).[24] In 1933 he composed an additional group of *papiers collés* based on drawings of newspaper advertisements. These inspired a series of fundamentally somber and vague canvases titled, simply, *Painting* (right). Miró painted the formally organic suggestions of these drawing-collages, which functioned as preliminary sketches, on top of those canvases. Quoting Miró and simultaneously invoking his magical sentiment, the artist and critic Ronald Penrose has explained that Miró employed shapes in this work as "signs that have no exact meaning" in much the same way the language of our ancestors did.[25] These abstract collages moved in the direction of the relief-collages that the poet George Hugnet denominated "objects," in which a distilled appeal to metonymy presented a challenge to art and opposed itself to good taste. One example of this is *The Spanish Dancer* (1928), a collage-object made with a pen, a cork, and a hat pin on cardboard. It can be considered the ultimate instance of those "sculptures or objects" of the years 1930–31 (p. 43, top) which Hugnet called "tragic and cruel toys."[26]

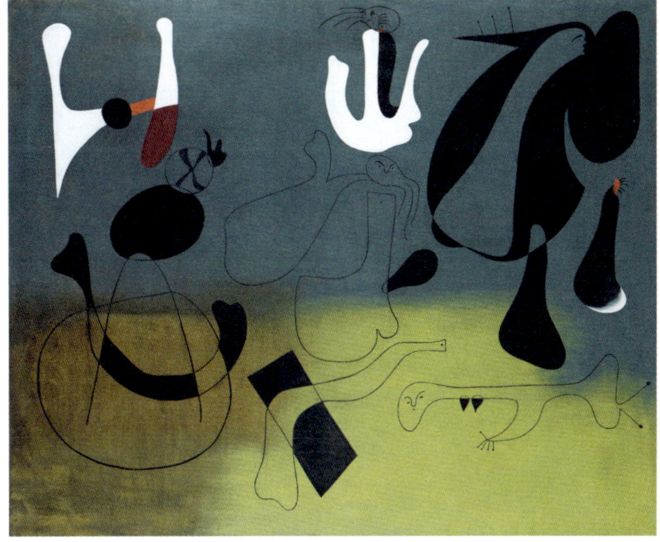

Peinture (Painting)
1933
Oil on canvas
51⅜ × 64⅛ in.
(130.5 × 163 cm)
Wadsworth Atheneum Museum of Art, Hartford, Connecticut. The Ella Gallup Sumner and Mary Catlin Sumner Collection Fund

Next Miró faced another challenge, one oriented toward a style of painting devoid of mimesis. This can be seen in series such as his abstract paintings on *Ingres* paper, composed in the summer of 1931, or in the ensemble of huge canvases published in 1930 by Georges Bataille in the periodical *Documents*. Of the latter collection Bataille especially valued *Painting (The Magic of Color)* (p. 42, top) for its radicalism with regard to terms like *tache* (mark), *informe* (formlessness), and the decomposition of painting.[27] Miró's artistic vocabulary, with its propensity for simplicity and contrast, negation of established compositional rules, and freedom of means and processes or interest in vigor of material, brought him closer to—while distancing him from—radical abstractionism at its peak.[28] His paintings of organic symbols with ties to the primitive, which George Hugnet related to prehistoric art, calligraphy, and ideograms,[29] and which would lead up to Miró's so-called *savage paintings* (1934–38), were an expression of the untamed and the destructive. This content justified their critical reception in the fields of lyrical abstraction and synthesis, something Miró shared with his artist friend Jean Arp and

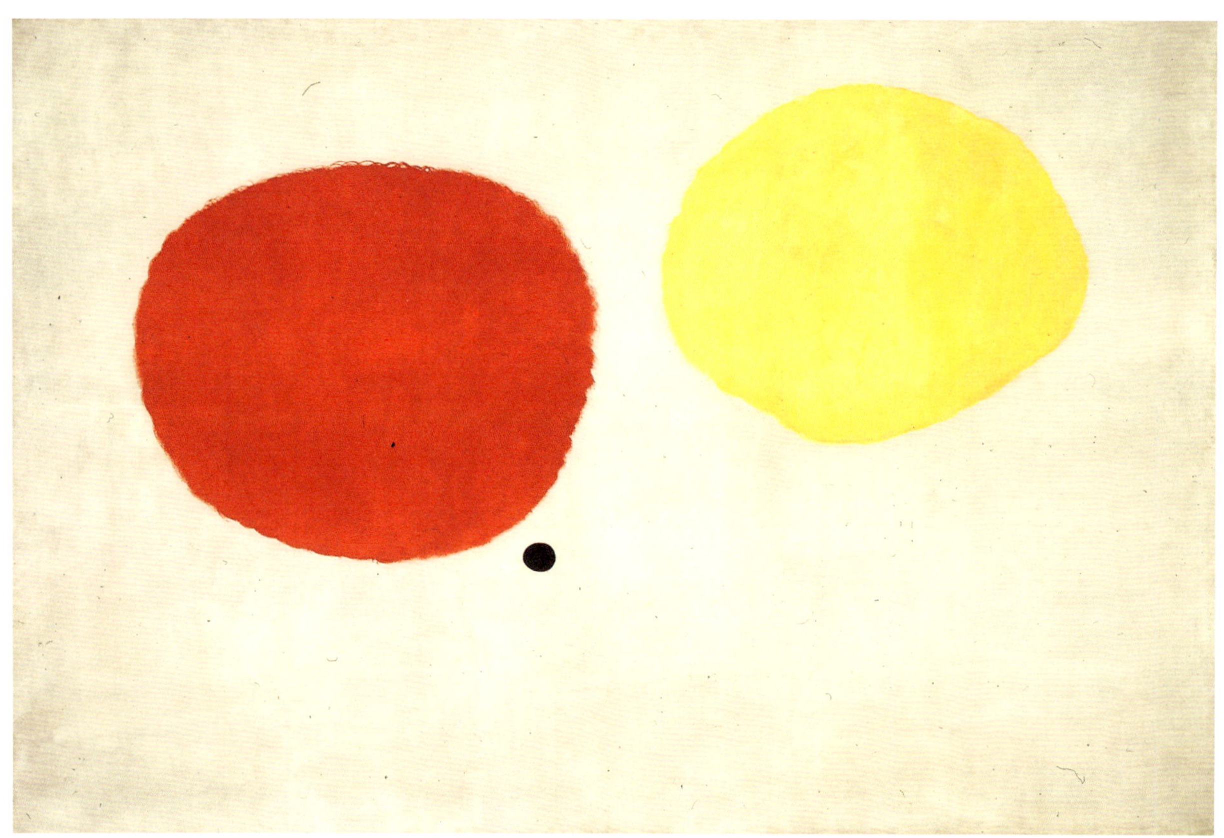

Peinture (La Magie de la couleur) (Painting [The Magic of Color])
1930
Oil on canvas
59⅛ × 88⅝ in.
(150.5 × 225 cm)
The Menil Collection, Houston

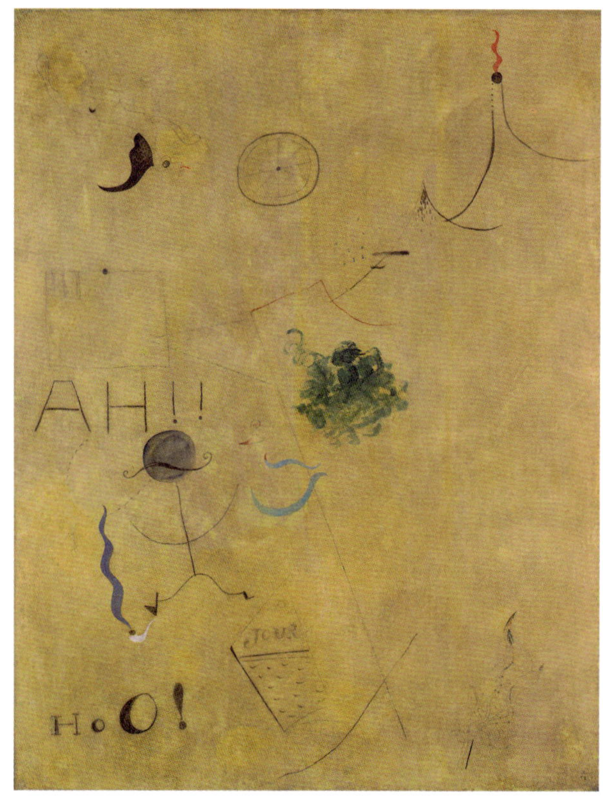

Le Renversement (The Somersault)
1924
Oil, pencil, charcoal, and tempera on canvas
36⅜ × 28¹¹⁄₁₆ in.
(92.4 × 72.8 cm)
Yale University Art Gallery, New Haven, Connecticut. Gift of Collection Société Anonyme

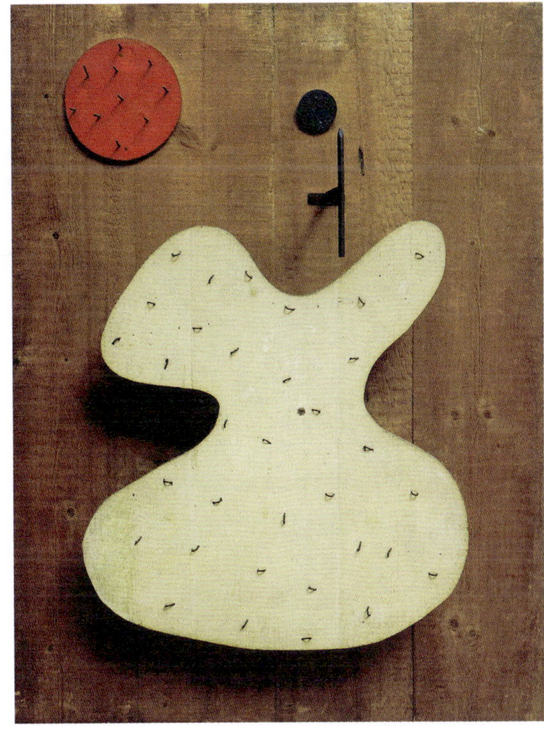

Relief Construction
Mont-roig,
August–November 1930
Wood and metal
35⅞ × 27⅝ × 6⅜ in.
(91.1 × 70.2 × 16.2 cm)
The Museum of Modern Art,
New York. Purchase

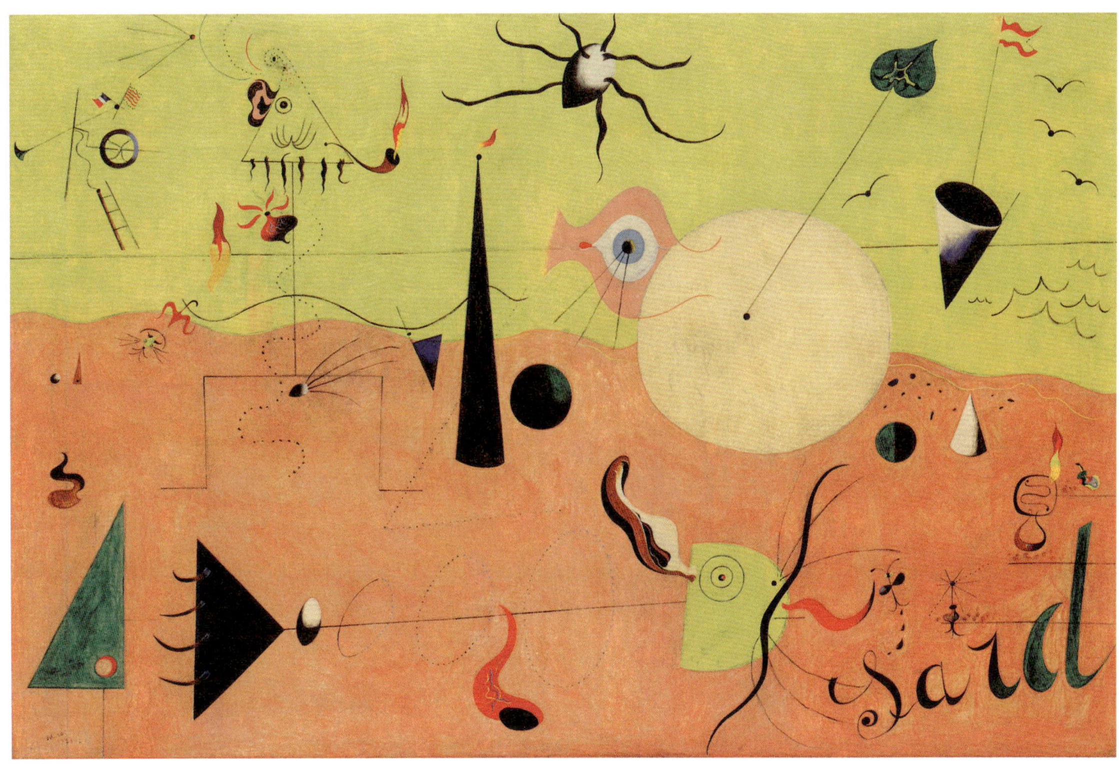

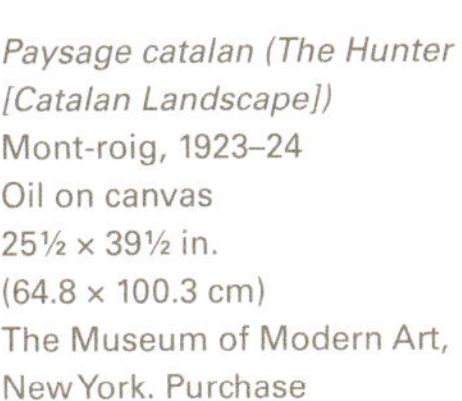

Paysage catalan (The Hunter [Catalan Landscape])
Mont-roig, 1923–24
Oil on canvas
25½ × 39½ in.
(64.8 × 100.3 cm)
The Museum of Modern Art,
New York. Purchase

with the painting pioneer Wassily Kandinsky, whom he met in 1933.[30] Anatole Jakovski, the critic for *Cahiers d'Art* who had close ties to Abstraction-Création,[31] identified Miró's pictorial universe with the expression of "the first and last pleasure of the soul's protoplasm," by means of "abstract forms that store memories" and the "fragile beauty of fragments."[32] He had anticipated the interpretation proposed by the *Thèse, antithèse, synthèse* exhibition catalog in 1935—in which the great *Painting* was included (p. 41)—which aligned him with the discontinuous extremes of abstraction, the opposite of the immutable absolute represented by Piet Mondrian.[33] This analysis acted as prelude to those maintained by New York's Museum of Modern Art's director Alfred H. Barr, Jr. in 1936[34] and by the British review *Axis*, which valued Miró's work as an example of the subjective form originating in Kandinsky's work.[35]

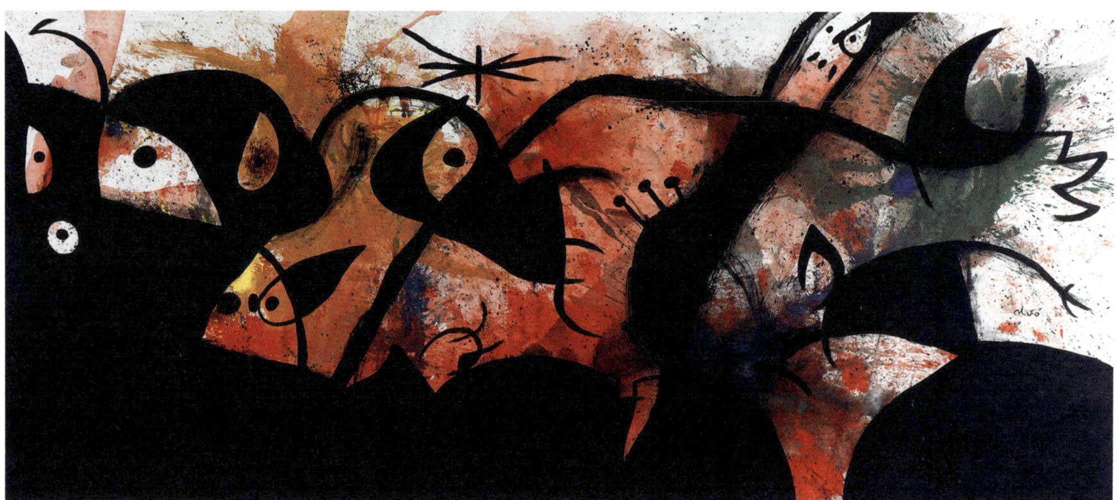

Personnages et oiseaux dans la nuit (Figures and Birds in the Night)
1974
Oil on canvas
108 × 250¾ in.
(274.5 × 637 cm)
Musée National d'Art Moderne, Centre Georges Pompidou, Paris, France

Miró's works offered American artists a type of painting that was linked to biomorphic abstraction as a symbol of nature's generative processes and opposed the predominant abstract Cubist tradition. The artist had an early presence in the United States, where Pierre Matisse's gallery began displaying his works in 1932.[36] They attracted the attention of collectors such as Katherine Dreier from the Société Anonyme,[37] for which she acquired *The Somersault* (1924) in 1927 (p. 42, bottom), and Alfred Eugene Gallatin, the founder of New York University's Gallery of Living Art, who since 1928 had bought many important works for the museum. James Johnson Sweeney, who had collaborated with the London-based periodical *Axis* and with Gallatin, organized a Miró retrospective at the Museum of Modern Art New York in 1941. This exhibition propelled appreciation of the artist's work down the path of an abstract painting with a compositional concept based in "an all-over disposition of flowing rhythms," as Sweeney called it,[38] and characterized by the expression of the emotional, which coincided with the contemporaneous claims of artists like Jackson Pollock, Arshile Gorky, and Mark Rothko.[39] Additionally, this reception was related to that of the *savage paintings*, which presented an alternative to modern painting in terms of political content at a time when the United States also considered itself to be directly involved in World War II.[40]

III.

The atmosphere of New York City, where Miró spent a period in 1947, was essential to the evolution of his work. It brought about a definitive shift in favor of the expression of the creative act itself. The imaginative fluidity of the gouaches in the *Constellations* series—with their expanded pictorial structure, understated backgrounds, and harmonic colors, all based on "the night, music, and the stars"[41]—had permitted him to surpass the connections between the reality depicted in his *savage paintings* through background structures based on transparencies and erosions of the surface, and a flat figuration, which banished both shape and chiaroscuro from his painting. This enabled him to take an unprecedented turn toward the spontaneous, which coincided with the demands of postwar art as the artist himself interpreted it. "New York," Miró remembered, "helped me to take stock of myself. I had to adapt myself to modernity. But that wasn't too difficult. I studied the counterpoint that emerged for the juxtaposition of brutal and spontaneous elements—as in my savage painting—between drawn forms and precisely painted ones. Around 1950 and 1951 I also painted canvases that were at times reflective—in which the work took precedence over the gesture—and at times impulsive, executed very rapidly, which were like mental vacations for me."[42] The French poet and art critic Jacques Dupin also made reference to Miró's contrasts between melody of line and counterpoint of color. He described the way the strokes came into place as a distillation of organic forms that conserved their vital energy. Color, made from fluid material, luminous and diurnal, offered a contrast that caused the composition, as Dupin has said, to resemble dodecaphonic music.[43]

At the peak of his career, Miró proposed sculpture as the great new site of innovation. His project in the thousand-year-old practice occupied one of the longest segments in his 1941 *Working Notes*. He had witnessed firsthand the radical syntactic innovations that the Modernist sculptors of the thirties had produced. Many of them, including Jean Arp, Max Ernst, Alberto Giacometti, Julio González, and Pablo Picasso, were his friends. About these relationships, he wrote: "When sculpting starts from the objects I collect, just as I make use of stain on paper and imperfections in canvases—do this here in the country in a way that is really alive, in touch with the elements of nature . . . make a cast of these objects and work on it like González does until the object as such no longer exists but becomes a sculpture, but not like Picasso—do it like a collage of various elements—the objects I have in Barcelona will not continue to exist as such but will become sculptures."[44] He set out to create a type of sculpture that resembled its original material less than it did González's metal constructions. He proposed a work based in collage that—as opposed to Picasso's method, where, with fierce and mimetic ingenuity, he had created the *Tête de taureau (Bull's Head)* (1942) from two bicycle parts cast in bronze—would serve to build interchangeable poetic metaphors, taking the vestiges of reality as a starting point.

This method was defined in terms of his old, magnetic, and fertile attraction to objects.[45] It resulted in an increased production of bronze sculptures, composed with the same lack of inhibition and radicalism with which he had conceived the structures of the thirties. Miró began to shape a trajectory through sculpture—he produced objects such as *Woman* (1946; p. 38), made of bones, metal, and stone. He also began to create his first sculptures in organic forms modeled on or derived from Arp or Picasso, such as the heavy and terrestrial *Moon Bird*, whose first bronze version is dated 1946–49. This evolution gave rise to a type of sculpture, temporally concentrated around the years 1967–74 and 1981, which synthesized the heterogeneity of the object and the uniformity of the cast, in addition to achieving his purpose of building a phantasmagorical world within real space.[46] Miró, who wrote, "I always have the Bible open when I am sculpting; that will give me a sense of grandeur and of gestation of the world,"[47] also devised a firm concept of the solemnity of the sacred.

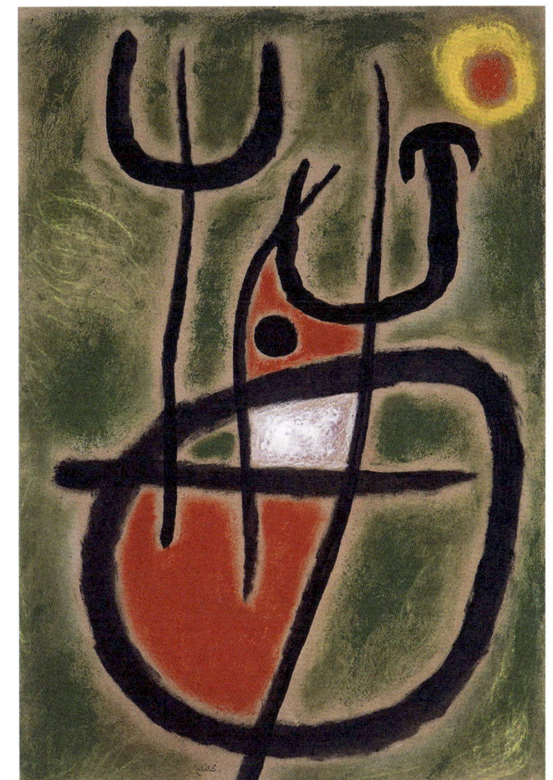

Personnage devant un paysage (Figure in Front of a Landscape)
1963
Mixed media on cardboard
41⁵⁄₁₆ × 29½ in. (105 × 75 cm)

Miró found the starting points for these sculptures in a varied repertoire of objects such as cans, pots, wood planks, trunks and branches, nails, clay, etc., which he collected and stored in his workshop. They functioned as interchangeable pieces that suggested continuous configurations, which the artist would capture in quick and accurate sketches.[48] They were finished by means of a two-phase artisanal procedure, in which the artist inscribed the wax mold by carving his own immutable symbols into it. He then used coarse and rough material (such as the rust of time and earth) for the final patina, which was completed at the Parellada Foundry in Barcelona.[49] One work that maintained its original artistic impulse was conceived

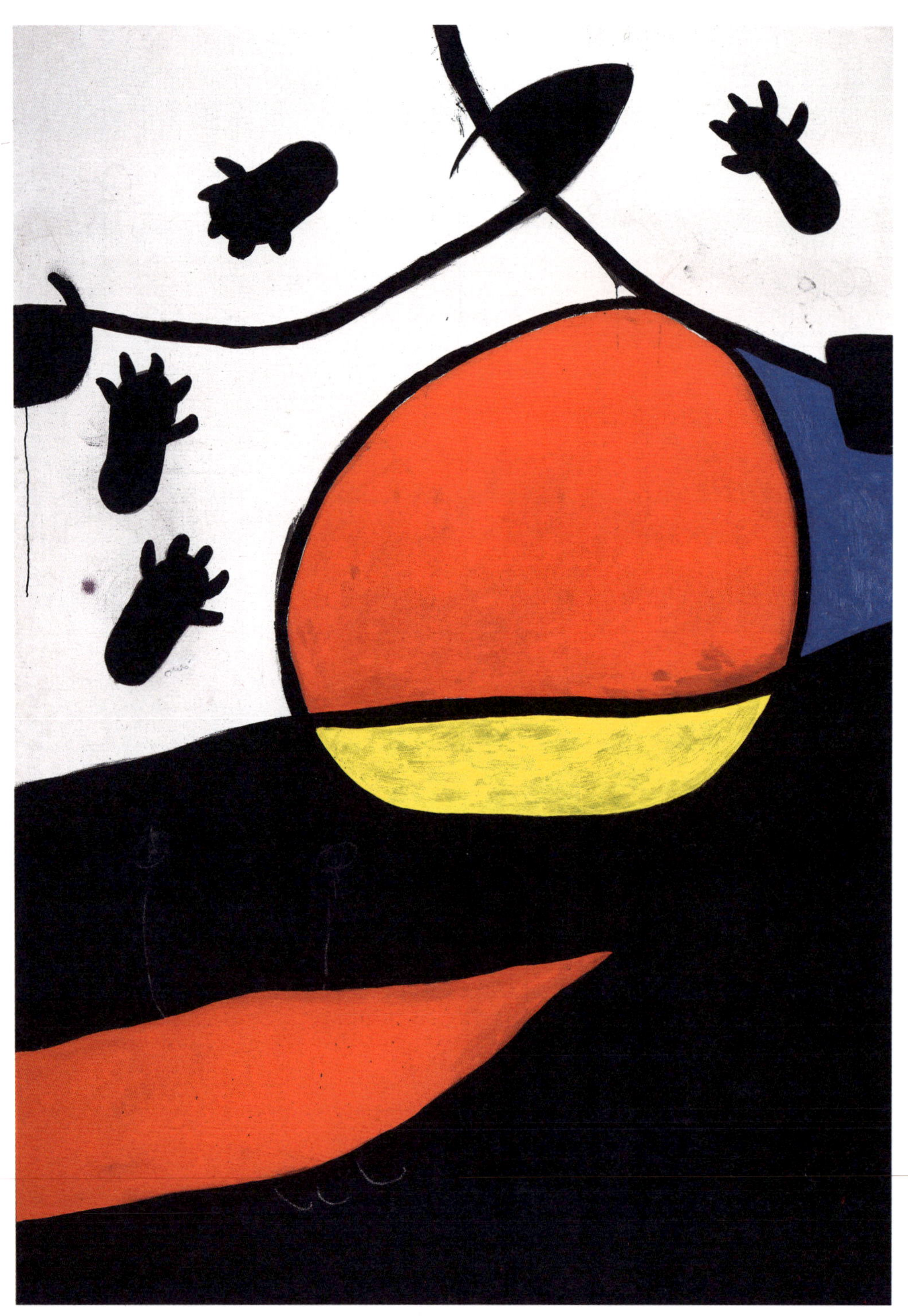

in 1933, when Joan Miró stated in an interview with *Minotaure*: "As for my means of expression, I struggle more and more to achieve the maximum clarity, power, and plastic [sculptural] aggressiveness; in other words, to provoke an immediate physical sensation that will then make its way to the soul."[50]

With these means of expression, starting in the sixties, the definitive codification of Miró's work finally took shape. It was a locus of meeting and metamorphosis in the sphere of double attraction, according to Dupin's expression, between cosmic forces and telluric impulses. The art critic Waldemar George had explained it in 1929 as the painting "of a physical vacuousness that easily balances out its interior magic," with ties to "cosmic sentiment" and the "intuition of mystery" seen in the ancestors, like those who painted the caves of Altamira, whom he specifically mentions on one hand, and to "incongruent paintings, brought to life by strange homunculi and fantastical plants,"[51] on the other. In this defining moment there came to be an encounter between the escape from spheres and the attraction to the abyss. Jacques Dupin elaborated: "there remains a space where things and beings can abide and encounter one another through a series of exchanges and metamorphoses, and this passing site is none other than the earth: neither sheltered from the risk from below, nor from the beckoning from above."[52]

Joan Miró had his repertory of immutable symbols: the woman representing the terrestrial and in opposition to the bird, a symbol of the imagination. Next to these were the themes of cosmic landscape and the constellations as structures of fluidity, universal beauty, and the human soul. With these symbols he developed his major and most mature works in accordance with the great expression of his "trajectory of the spirit." Later paintings were characterized by slow conception and detailed creation, such as the great *Woman, Bird and Star (Homage to Picasso)* (1966–73; p. 4). This canvas was heir to the pure colors and clearly defined imaginary objects that Miró had identified in 1947 with his monumental painting for the Hotel Terrace Place in Cincinnati. It made use of a splendid fragmented background that left visible traces of its preparation and contrasted them with the smooth delineation of figures that suggest an escape. Other works were characterized by freer expression in which the foundation lacked preparation. One such work is *Figure in Front of a Landscape* (1963; p. 45), which belonged to a series created on cardboard between 1959 and 1965. Here the figure was composed of lively black brushstrokes, while those elements rendered in color were related to a landscape connected to the cosmos. The figure in front of the landscape was composed by means of a graphic system as essential as that of this canvas, and shared an artistic intention with various sculptures. The 1967 work *Young Girl* (p. 10), for example, is made of three planks of wood, a nail, a dollop of mud, and a broken rake. Similarly, the monumental—despite its diminutive size—*Woman at the Square in a Cemetery* (1981; p. 85) was fashioned from cardboard boxes, wood beams, and the sculpted figure of the bird woman.

Paysage (Landscape)
1974
Acrylic and chalk on canvas
96¹⁄₁₆ × 67½ in.
(244 × 171.5 cm)

The beautiful canvas *Women VI* (p. 29), the last in the series *Women and Birds* from 1969, represents the direct expression of an active energy. Miró attained this expression starting in 1953, with works such as the great canvas *Painting* for the Solomon R. Guggenheim Museum. In small formats, Miró accomplished the same expansion of a background covered with mixed colors on top of a rough-hewn support, which creates the sensation of a whirlwind throughout the space of the painting. The canvas is sprinkled with smudges, blurs, drips, or various other material accidents. Wide black strokes form curves over an energetic space, alluding to the feminine figure and the flight of birds. They also intensely express a poetic longing of the figure and the liberating energy of the painter. This electric and fluid movement of forms corresponded to the intrinsically dynamic configuration, in its instability, of a later sculpture, *Dancer* (1981; p. 73, top). The lightness of its style is reminiscent of the painting *Woman, Birds* (1972; p. 51), in which the ample figure of a seated woman is placed in counterpoint to the flight of birds over a shapeless space achieved by a very blurred painting style. That style perpetuates the attribute of understanding of the active void that Michel Leiris had attributed to the Oneiric Paintings. They had, he wrote, "the appearance of being more smeared than painted, sordid like destroyed buildings, seductive like faded walls, . . . mysterious poems."[53]

In 1959, before finishing the first of the monochromatic triptychs, which Margit Rowell linked to the sense of absolute fulfillment and the impersonal nature of Mallarmé,[54] Miró had declared: "Immobility makes me think of vast spaces that contain movements that do not stop, movements that have no end. As Kant said, it is a sudden irruption of the infinite into the finite. A pebble, which is a finite and immobile object, suggests not only movement to me but movement that has no end. In my paintings, this translates into the spark-like forms that leap out of the frame, as though from a volcano."[55] The spatial paintings, such as *Poem to the Glory of Sparkles* (1969; p. 61), and the empty canvases *The Dance of the*

Poppies (1973; p. 80), *Bird in Space* (1976; pp. 81–83), and *Landscape* (1976; p. 79) represent, through their magnificent and diversely treated white backgrounds, the poetic idea of a scintillating universe and an immobile movement that moved the artist. In his sculpture they offered, in their material fragility, the beautiful invention titled *Young Woman Dreaming of Evasion* (1969; p. 73, bottom). It is constructed on a base of round stones, clay, and rods, like a symbol of perpetual motion and the human being's infinite will to escape (which is evoked by the rising rhythm of the figure). A parallel metaphor is presented in those sculptures that unify figure and cosmos, such as the delicate *Woman with Beautiful Breasts* (1969; p. 22), from the same year. Here the elemental imaginative form of the circle constitutes both a head and the sexual attribute which lends the work its title. It manages to be as light as the whole sculpture, which seems to be made up of the dissociated elements of a landscape without losing its anthropomorphic quality. Another example is the stylized 1966 figure, *Sun Woman* (p. 20), of a more static quality, which was based on a phantasmagorical union of a broken clay pot, a branch, and figures modeled in clay.

The presence of *gravitas*, that concept of the black and telluric, continued to grow in works defined by a vastly liberated energy. This is evident in various 1974 canvases such as *Spanish Woman* (p. 19), *Figure, Birds* (p. 33), and 1977's *Bird Woman I* (p. 64) and *Bird Woman II* (p. 27), as well as the impressive and furiously rendered drawing *Woman, Figure, Bird* (1973–77; p. 15). These works demonstrate the gestural energy in which Miró submerged himself after his last trip to the United States in 1968, and that, like this last work, encouraged him to mix media and processes in a way that would demonstrate the importance of the materials and the radical creative act in the paintings of his last years (p. 44). The same attraction to the terrestrial and to blackness, which acted as night as well as a primitive melting pot, appeared in Miró's sculpture. See, for example, the terrestrial figures of 1968, *Woman* (p. 23), born of the extended form of an anchor or harpoon covered in mud, and *Figure* (p. 37), based on the imprint of a footprint in the mud, or the round and telluric *Bull's Head* (1970; p. 35), or *The Warrior King* (1981; cover image). All of these works are connected to the figure seated on the hunter's land from Miró's earliest canvases, now with a brutal aspect.

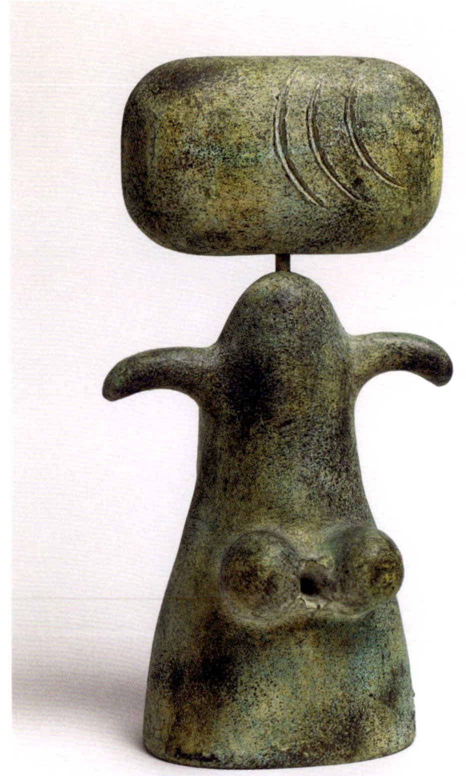

These are examples of the constant turmoil of Miró's visual thought, under the continuous control of form, which led him to create these imaginary beings in a hybrid space. In this space melancholy takes on a human form, in perpetual precariousness due to its earthly condition—as in the moving canvas *Woman Entranced by the Escape of Shooting Stars* (1969; p. 18). In 1974, Miró linked the universe of these artistic-poetic configurations to the mysterious and fertile creative act, declaring: "For me, the essential things are the artistic and poetic occurrences, the association of forms and ideas: a form gives me an idea, this idea evokes another form, and everything culminates in figures, animals, and things I had no way of foreseeing in advance."[56]

TRANSLATED BY EMILY THOMPSON

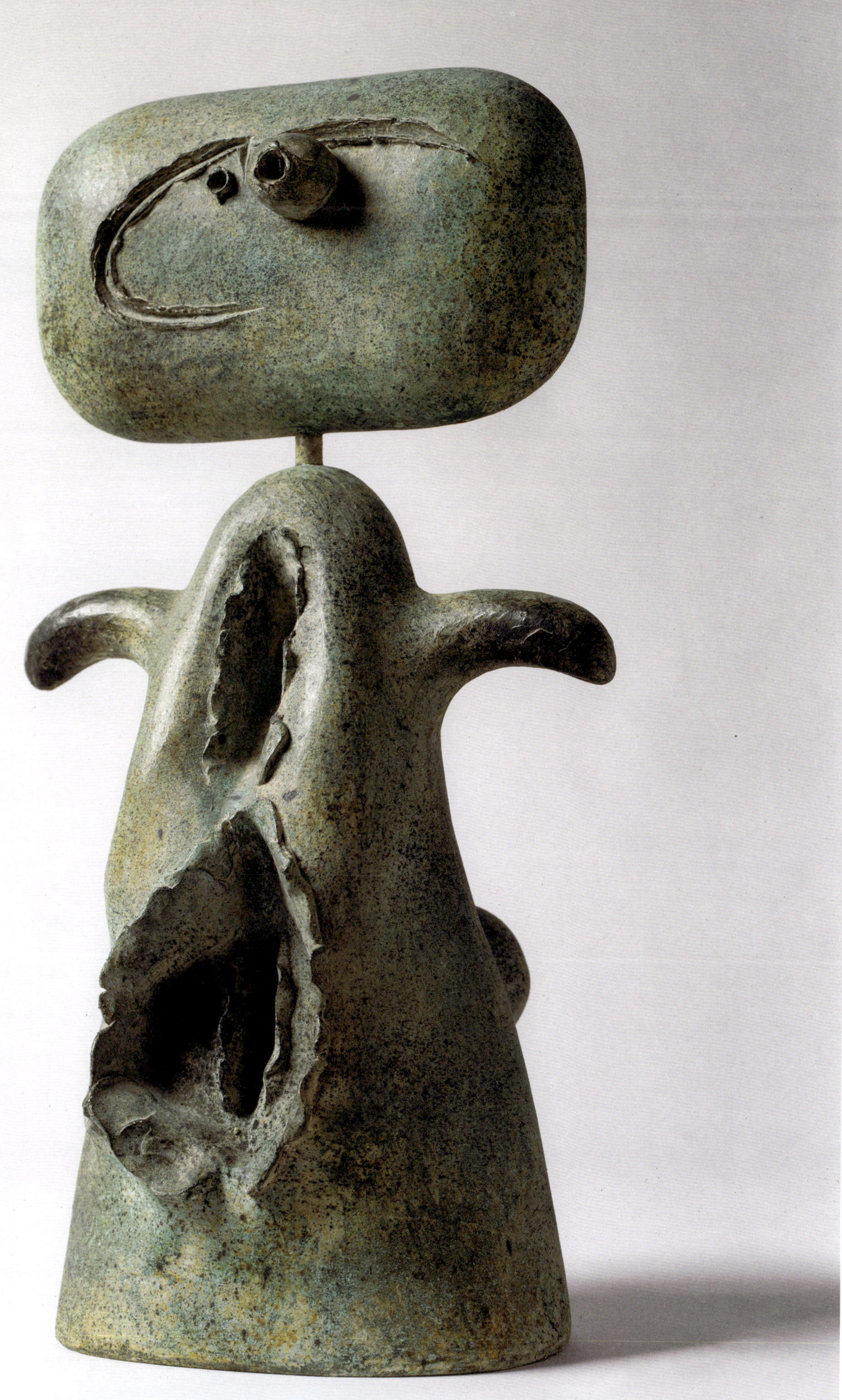

Femme (Woman)
1981
Patinated bronze
21¼ × 11⁷⁄₁₆ × 8¹¹⁄₁₆ in.
(54 × 29 × 22 cm)

Back view on opposite page.

1. Joan Miró, "Working Notes, 1941–42," in *Joan Miró: Selected Writings and Interviews*, ed. Margit Rowell (London: Thames and Hudson, 1987), 185–86.

2. Waldemar George, "Miró et le miracle ressuscité," *Le Centaure* (Brussels) 3, no. 8 (1929): 201–4. Spanish version in *El descubrimiento de Miró. Miró y sus críticos, 1918–1929*, ed. Victoria Combalia (Barcelona: Ediciones Destino, 1990): 226.

3. Due to the war in France, Miró had been living in Varengeville-sur-Mer beginning in 1939. In May of 1940 he decided to return to Spain and moved to Palma de Mallorca. In June 1941 he resumed his old habit of spending the summer months in Mont-roig (Tarragona), the Catalonian town he had been visiting since 1911 and in which he had lived during the outbreak of the Spanish Civil War in July 1936. In February 1942, the painter moved to Barcelona, while continuing to spend his summers in Mont-roig. In 1948 he began spending seasons in Paris and finally, in 1956, Miró settled into the studio established by Josep Lluís Sert in Son Abrines, Palma de Mallorca.

4. Joan Miró, "Notas de trabajo, 1940–41," in *Joan Miró. Escritos y conversaciones*, ed. Margit Rowell (Murcia, Spain: Valencia, 2002): 246–47.

5. See "Comments by Joan Miró" by Rosamond Bernier, *L'Oeil* (Paris) 79/80 (1961): 12, in Rowell, *Joan Miró. Escritos*, 257.

6. See Joan Miró, "Statement," in "A chacun sa realité," P. Volboudt, *XX Siècle* 5, no. 9 (1957): 24, in Rowell, *Joan Miró: Selected Writings*, 240.

7. Miró to J. F. Ràfols, 26 September 1923, in Rowell, *Joan Miró: Selected Writings*, 82: "I am working really a lot, with absolute regularity and method. . . . This year I am really attacking the landscape, when I need to relax, still lifes. . . . I have already managed to break absolutely free of nature and the landscapes have nothing whatever to do with outer reality."

8. In 1925 Joan Miró abandoned fantastic figures in favor of a style that Pierre Daix, the greatest expert in his work, has designated the "Oneiric Paintings." They are a group of paintings finished in Paris between 1925 and 1927 in which, absent descriptive details, the forms seem to emanate from a void. These paintings had an oneiric, or dreamy, atmosphere and were almost monochromatic, with allusive and suggestive lines based on smudges and lightly rendered forms. Some of these paintings are referenced in Michel Leiris's much noted article in the fifth issue of *Documents*, a dissident Surrealist art magazine, in 1929.

9. The building housed Masson's and Miró's studios, which attracted, at different times, writers such as Antonin Artaud, Georges Limbour, Arman Salacroy, Roland Tual, Robert Desnos, and Michel Leiris. The magazine *Littérature* provided a connection to the official Surrealist movement. See Michel Leiris, "45, rue Blomet," *Zébrage* (Paris: Gallimard, 1992): 219; Joan Miró, "Memories of the rue Blomet," 1977, in Rowell, *Joan Miró: Selected Writings*, 99–104; and Robert Desnos ["Joan Miró"], *Cahiers d'Art*, nos. 1–4 (1934): 25–26.

10. Miró to Michel Leiris, 8 October 1924, in Rowell, *Joan Miró: Selected Writings*, 86. "In leafing through my notebook I have also noticed the extremely disturbing quality of the dissociated drawings I sometimes do—meant for canvases I am preparing and on which I jot down a number of remarks . . . I agree with Breton that there is something extremely disturbing about a page of writing."

11. See Joan Miró, "Statement," in *Minotaure*, December 1933, in Rowell, *Joan Miró: Selected Writings*, 122.

12. See Maurice Raynal, *Anthologie de la peinture en France de 1906 à nos jours* (Paris: Éditions Montaigne, 1927): 34, 36–37, 237–38.

13. See André Breton, *Le Surréalisme et la Peinture*, 2nd rev. ed. (Paris: Gallimard, 1965): 36–37.

14. In 1941, Breton stated that Miró's "tumultuous entry" into Surrealism had taken place in 1924. See Breton, *Genèse et perspective artistiques du surréalisme* (1941) in Breton, *Le Surréalisme et la Peinture*, 70.

15. In his preface to Miró's 1925 exhibition in the Pierre Loeb Gallery in Paris, Benjamin Péret noted the importance of Klee's painting as a part of the search for poetry and emotion. See Alain Jouffroy, *Miró* (Paris: Ed. Fernand Hazan, 1987): 49. In a conversation with Brassaï in 1955, Miró noted: "Klee was the best thing I ever found. It was under his influence that my painting freed itself from all terrestrial ties, Klee has made me understand that a stain, an exhalation, or even a point can be a pictorial theme, just the same as a face, a landscape, or a monument." Brassaï, *Les artistes de ma vie* (Paris: Editions Denoël, 1982): 143.

16. See Miró, "Memories of the rue Blomet," in Rowell, *Joan Miró: Selected Writings*, 103.

17. See note 9.

18. See Leiris, "45, rue Blomet," 227.

19. Joan Miró, "Comment and Interview," by James Johnson Sweeney, *Partisan Review*, no. 2 (1948): 206–12, in Rowell, *Joan Miró: Selected Writings*, 208–9: "until, in 1925, I was drawing almost entirely from hallucinations . . . little by little I turned from depend[ing] on hallucinations to forms suggested by physical elements."

20. See Robert Desnos, "Peinture surréaliste," *Zürcher Zeitung*, October 25, 1929, in Combalia, *El descubrimiento de Miró*, 265.

21. The schism became final in December 1929, when Breton published the Second Surrealist Manifesto. A few months before, Bataille had founded the magazine *Documents*, whose first issue was released in April. Many of the Rue Blomet group's members had taken refuge in this publication after abandoning the official Surrealism.

22. In 1931 the poet Georges Hugnet used this concept to describe the abstract painting and objects made by Miró. He referred to his art as "the purest," in which he wrote: "infancy traces the symbol," a visual symbol that represents "the infancy of the first man and of all men," a "cave symbol." See Hugnet, "Joan Miró ou l'enfance de l'art," *Cahiers d'Art*, nos. 7–8 (1931): 337. The relationship between the idea of the primitive and the infantile state of man was transmitted through the magazine *Documents*, in which Bataille wrote about Luquet's anthropological theory and about Miró's paintings, which he published as an expression of the primitive and the anti-pictorial. See Felix Fanés, *Pintura, collage, cultura de masas. Joan Miró, 1919–1934*, Alianza Editorial, Madrid, 2007 (pp. 191–96).

23. See Louis Aragon, *Exposition de Collages. La peinture au défi* (Paris: Librairie Corti, 1930): 10–12. [Monograph published for the exhibition at the Galerie Goermans]: He distinguishes between two types of collage: those based in form and those tied to their materials; both are more closely connected to magic than to painting.

24. See ibid. pp. 26–27, ills. XVIII, XIX. As Louis Aragon noticed in 1930, Miró's material movement toward collage was preceded by Picasso, whose two large collages titled *Guitare* in 1926 were published that year in *Cahiers d'Art*, and later (one of them) in monograph format.

25. See Roland Penrose, *Miró* (London: Thames and Hudson, 1970): 76–77. The first avant-garde artists' fascination with African and Oceanic art, and later Pre-Columbian cultures and medieval European art—was based on an attraction to their concise and abstract forms, as well as the magical interpretation of their meaning.

26. See Hugnet, "Joan Miró ou l'enfance de l'art," 339.

27. See Georges Bataille, "Joan Miró: Peintures récentes," *Documents*, no. 7 (1930): 399.

28. Georges Duthuit, "Où allez-vous Joan Miró," *Cahiers d'Art*, nos. 8–10 (1936): 261–64. Reproduced in Rowell, *Joan Miró: Selected Writings*, 151–52: "Have you ever heard of anything more stupid than 'abstraction-abstraction'. And they ask me into their deserted house, as if the marks I put on a canvas did not correspond to a concrete representation of my mind, did not possess a profound reality."

29. See Hugnet, "Joan Miró ou l'enfance de l'art," 336.

30. See Jessica Boissel, *Kandinsky-Albers. Une correspondance des années trente*, Les Cahiers du Musée National D'art Moderne, Hors-série/Archives (Paris: Centre Georges Pompidou, 1998): 89 [letter dated 15 November 1936, in which Kandinsky definitively separates Miró from the Surrealists and expresses interest in his painting].

31. Abstraction-Création was formed by Theo van Doesburg and fellow artists in 1931 to reassert the importance of abstract painting and to counteract André Breton's influential positions on Surrealism.

32. Anatole Jakovski, ["Joan Miró"], *Cahiers d'Art*, nos. 1–4 (1934): 58.

33. See Anatole Jakovski, "Paris," in *Thèse, antithèse, synthèse*, ed. Paul Hilber, S. Giedion, Jean Hélion, Anatole Jakovski, W. Kandinsky, and James Johnson Sweeney (Lucerne, Switzerland: Kunstmuseum Luzern, 1935): 12–13. Exhibition catalog.

34. See Alfred H. Barr Jr., *Cubism and Abstract Art* (New York: The Museum of Modern Art, 1936): 12–13 and 19 [Exhibition catalog]: Barr distinguished between *Pure-abstractions* and *Near-abstractions*, including Arp and Miró in the latter.

35. See J. Thwaites and M. Thwaites, "Surrealism and Abstraction—The Search for Subjective Form," in *Axis. A Quarterly Review of Contemporary "Abstract" Painting & Sculpture* (London), no. 6 (1936): 21–25.

36. In 1945 this gallery exhibited the *Constellations* series.

37. Founded in 1920 by Katherine Dreier, Man Ray and Marcel Duchamp, the organization promoted avant-garde art through exhibitions, lectures, publications, and concerts.

38. James Johnson Sweeney, *Joan Miró* (New York: Museum of Modern Art, 1941): 29–30. Exhibition catalog.

39. See Barbara Rose, *Miró in América* (Houston: The Museum of Fine Art, 1982): 19–20. Exhibition catalog.

40. Ibid., 37: Suggests that Miró was a model of antifascist resistance, as well as an example of the synthesis of form and psychological content. Rose cites an article by Georges L. K. Morris in the *Partisan Review* in 1938, in addition to Clement Greenberg's 1948 book.

41. See James Johnson Sweeney, "Joan Miró, Comment and Interview," *Partisan Review*, no. 2 (1948): 206–12, in Rowell, *Joan Miró: Selected Writings*, 208–9.

42. Joan Miró, "Miró," in Denys Chevalier, *Aujourd'hui: Art et architecture* 7, no. 39 (1962): 6–13, in Rowell, *Joan Miró: Selected Writings*, 269.

43. See Jacques Dupin, *Miró* (Paris: Flammarion, 1993): 265 and 304. Translated into English as *Miró*, 2nd ed. (New York: Harry N. Abrams, 1993).

44. Joan Miró, "Working Notes, 1941–42," in Rowell, *Joan Miró: Selected Writings*, 175.

45. Miró to Pierre Matisse, Barcelona, 28 September 1936, in Rowell, *Joan Miró: Selected Writings*, 126: "I feel myself attracted by a *magnetic* force toward an object, and then I feel

myself being drawn toward another object which is added to the first, and their combination creates a poetic shock—not to mention their original formal physical impact—which makes the poetry truly moving, and without which it would have no effect."

46. Miró, "Working Notes, 1941–42," in Rowell, *Joan Miró: Selected Writings*, 175: "It is in sculpture that I will create a truly phantasmagorical world of living monsters . . . the sculptures must resemble living monsters who live in the studio—a world apart . . . may my sculpture be confused with elements of nature, trees, rocks, roots, mountains, plants, flowers."

47. Ibid., 190.

48. These have been largely conserved at the Fundación Pilar y Joan Miró de Palma de Mallorca.

49. The shaping and final definition of Miró's bronze sculptures took place between the Son Boter workshop, where he stored found objects while awaiting the birth of the character he had devised, and the smelting workshop in Barcelona where, with the artist's active input, the work was transformed into its definitive bronze version. This process was described by Jacques Dupin in an illustrated volume with photographs taken at the foundry by Catalá-Roca (*Miró as Sculptor*, Ediciones Polígrafa, Barcelona, 1976; Spanish edition, 1972). Dupin wrote: "It all begins with an unpremeditated havesting. Miró slips out of his studio like a shadow and comes back laden down like a pack-horse. Laden with all sorts of things—valueless, obsolete, but capable in his eyes of unexpected associations and metamorphoses. . . . Objects thrown away and fragments of nature pile up in the studio, waiting to be joined together. The work of assembly, on the floor, is rough, irreverent and approximate. Miró, with artless audacity, takes very little trouble to restrain the forms, inflect the lines, modify the volumes or specify the articulation. . . . For years the objects garnered by Miró serve their sentences, languishing in the room with the closed shutters in Son Boter. Then comes a day when they can stand it no longer and they revolt against their jailer. And one instant of illumination, after that endless night, is enough for a sculpture to spring fully armed from the chaos of the studio. Yet another character to cross the sea and enter the furnace of the Paseo Turull."

50. Rowell, *Joan Miró: Selected Writings*, 122.

51. Combalia, *El descubrimiento de Miró*, 227.

52. Dupin, *Miró*, 351.

53. Michel Leiris, "Joan Miró," *Documents* (Paris), no. 5 (October 1929).

54. See Margit Rowell, *Joan Miró. Peinture-Poesie* (Paris: Éditions de la différence, 1976): 105.

55. Joan Miró, "I Work like a Gardener," interview by Yvon Taillandier, 15 February 1959, in Rowell, *Joan Miró: Selected Writings*, 248.

56. Joan Miró, "Miró: Now I Work on the Floor," interview by Yvon Taillandier, 30 May 1974, in Rowell, *Joan Miró: Selected Writings*, 284.

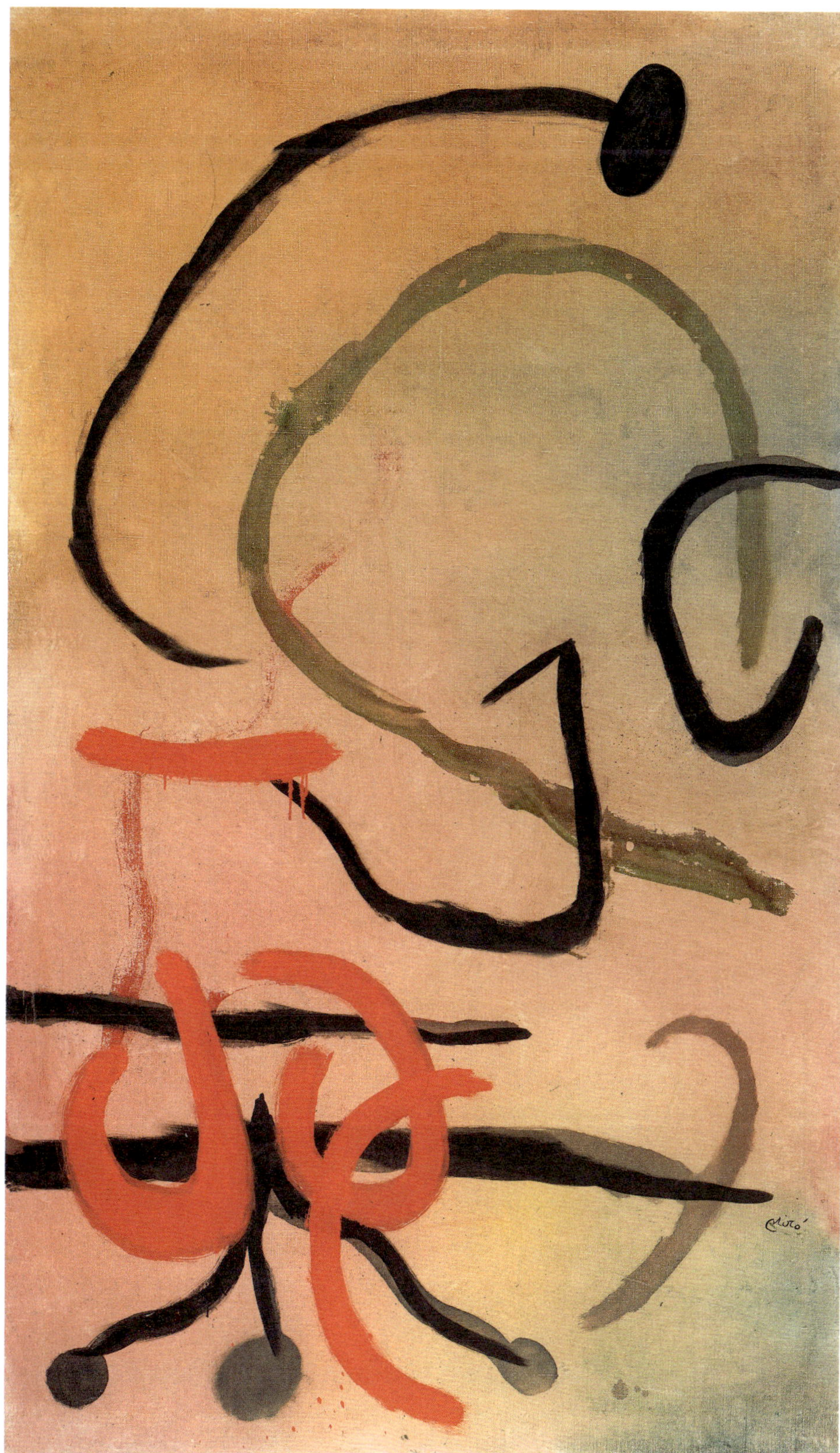

Femme, oiseaux (Woman, Birds), 1972, oil and acrylic on canvas, 64 × 38$\frac{3}{16}$ in. (162.5 × 97 cm)

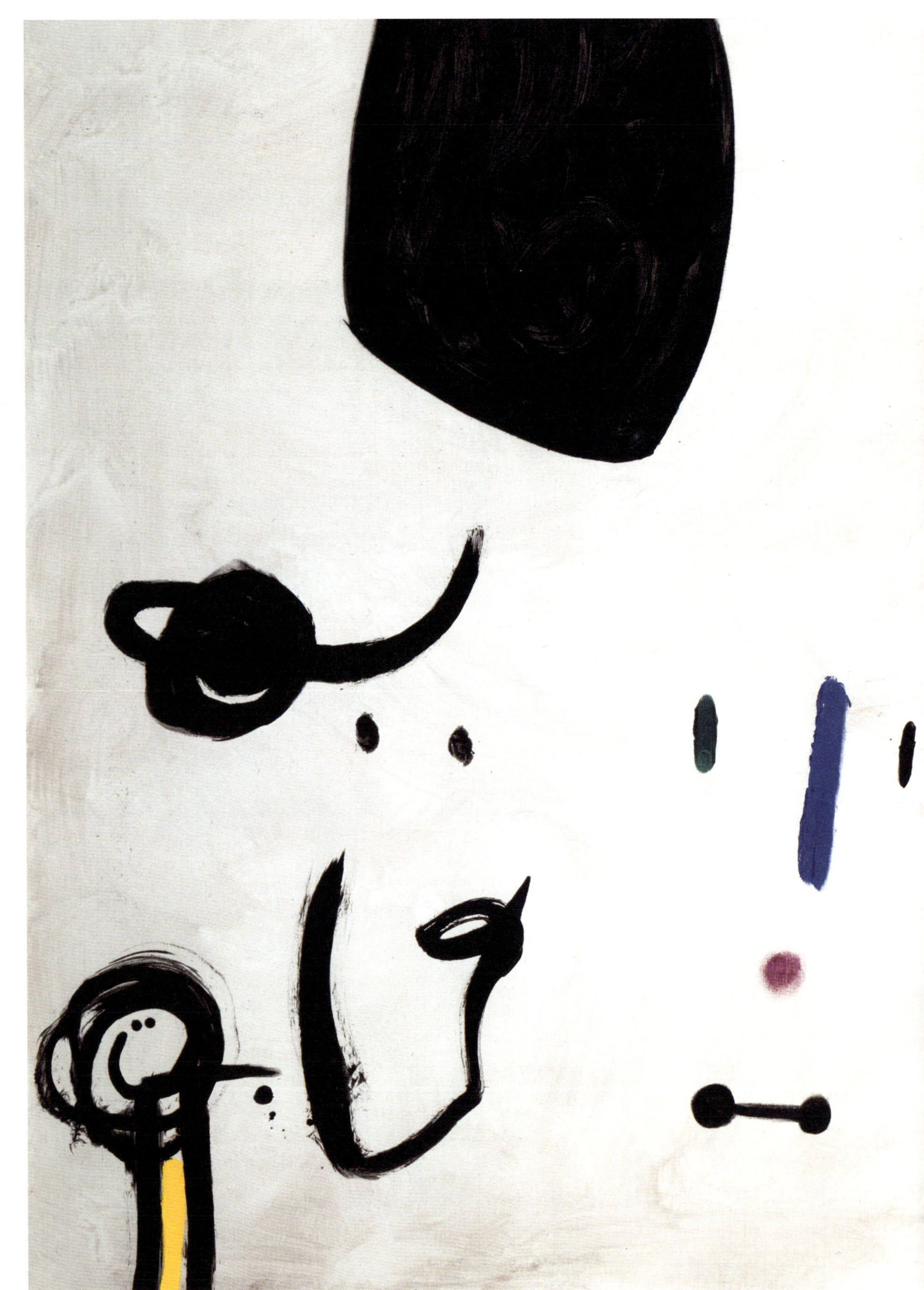

Paysage (Landscape), 1976, oil and acrylic on canvas, 51 3/16 × 76 9/16 in. (130 × 194.5 cm). Detail on following page.

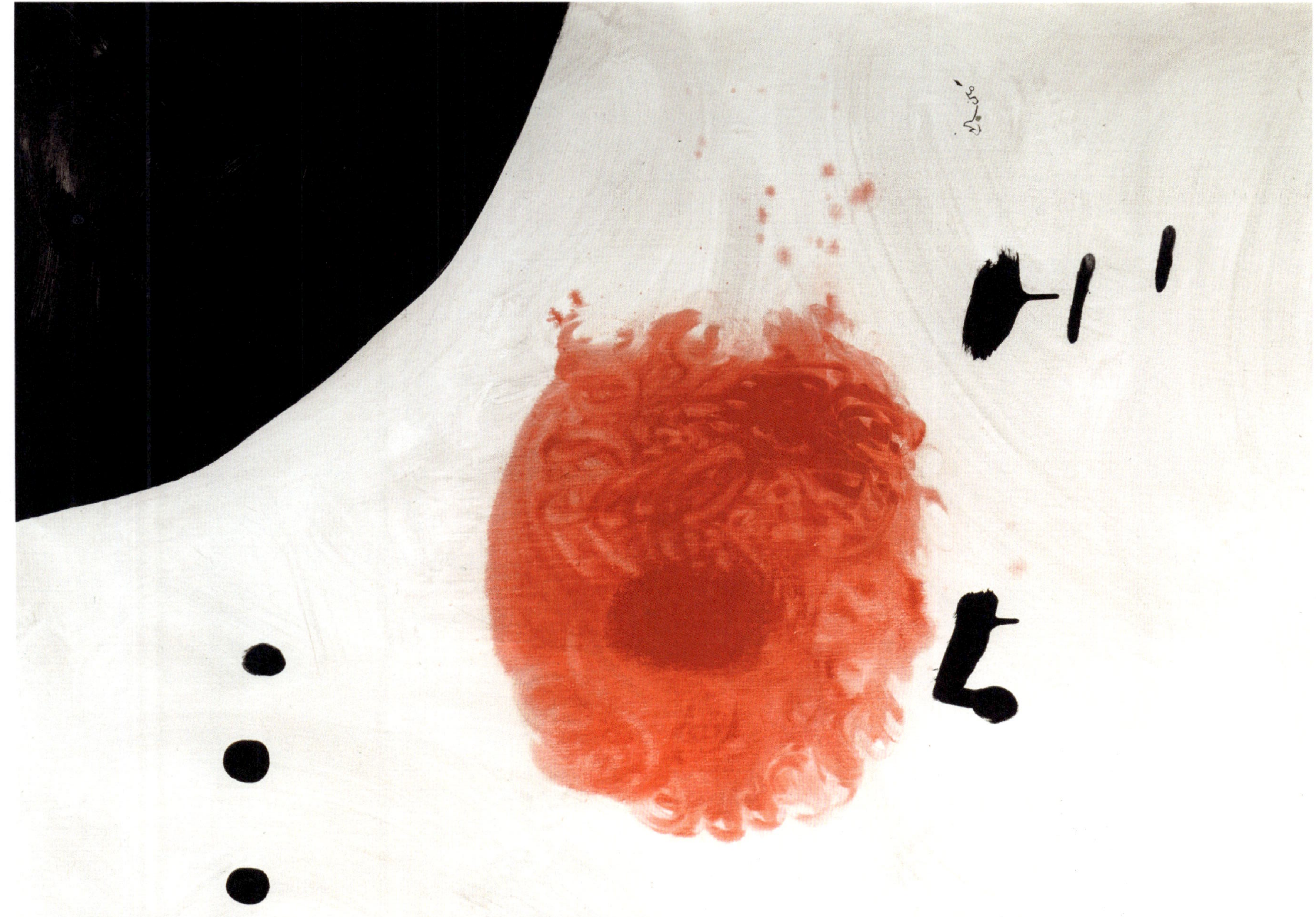

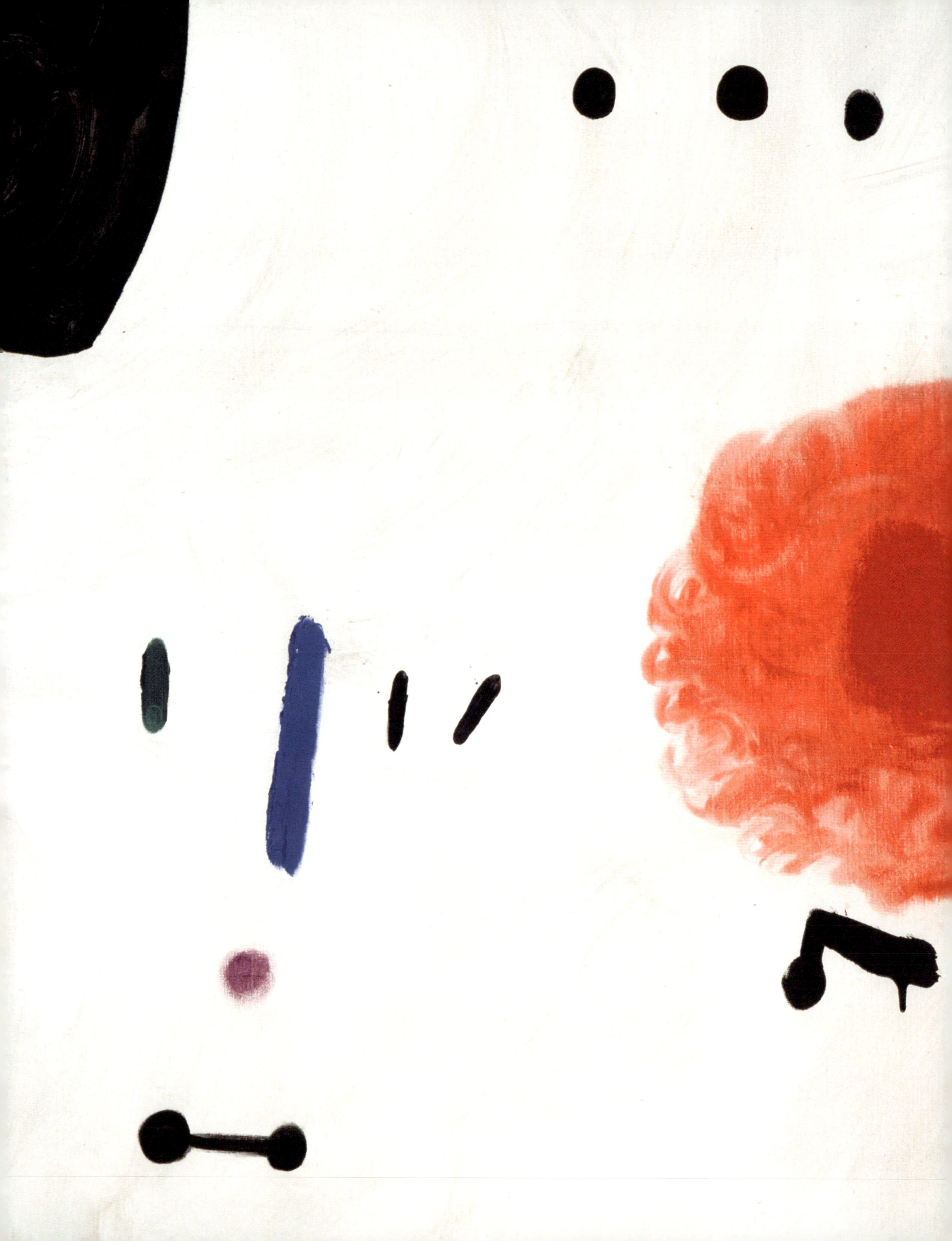

Miró Projects

Charles Palermo

While Joan Miró was in New York in 1947, Marcel Duchamp gave him a birthday gift, a necktie decorated with an image of a rearing horse. Duchamp signed and dated the tie's reverse, thereby making it, in the estimation of the poets Jacques Dupin and Jean Suquet, not just a tie or a gift, but a readymade. As it happens, a necktie figures in the *The Bride Stripped Bare by Her Bachelors, Even (The Large Glass)* (1915–23). A sheet of notes from the *Green Box* (a limited edition of facsimiles Duchamp produced in 1934 as a kind of explanation for his masterpiece) labeled the painting's necktie "a sort of principal form on which the composition as a whole rests."[1] Dupin and Suquet later assert: "A necktie, the ugliest ornament behind which men hide their nudity, but it links the sky and the earth. At least in the Large Glass!"[2] Furthermore, they see it as connecting, in the absence of a way to represent the fourth dimension—i.e., time—directly, "yesterday, today, tomorrow."[3] In short, the necktie can be taken as a link not just between heaven and earth, but between past and present, as well. The retrospective gesture of Duchamp's gift to Miró, creating a 1947 readymade from the *Large Glass* project, mirrors this same pair of connections in space and time.

This story may help us understand the relation of Miró's achievement to the history of modern painting, even the history of art. I suggest we reconsider Miró's late work and its relation to history in terms of a *retrospective temporality*. Try, if you will, to think of Miró's work, in its relation to time and to history, the way we are already accustomed to thinking of Duchamp's. Duchamp made new works out of a retrospective relation to historical works of art. Their status as works of art depends on their relation to prior projects and already-existing objects. We will see that the same goes for Miró.

Miró's work, and especially the late work which forms the present exhibition, should be seen with Duchamp's avant-gardist gestures for two reasons: Duchamp's consequence in Miró's life and an opposition between absence and literal presence. Duchamp was an influential example to Miró and a significant supporter, a role that is easily overlooked. Moreover, the kind of retrospective temporality that characterizes Duchamp's oeuvre becomes an important feature of Miró's from the 1950s on. I have argued elsewhere that Miró's work, even from its beginnings, opposed the absent—the past or the distant—world of the picture to the literal presence of the work itself, bringing the two into a near-identity that also declares their difference.

In order to understand Miró's late work *as late work*, we must learn how he adapts a retrospective temporality like Duchamp's to his reflection on his own career. He comes to consider his own career as a kind of institution, an edifice in the art world, of the kind that the avant-gardist rejects. In other words, Miró's late work takes up Miró's own career as the absence it opposes to that effect of presence that is his hallmark. These issues are in the very fabric and paint of these late works.

MIRÓ WITHIN MODERN ART

Miró's earliest work—up to the mid twenties—fits into a narrative of modernist apprenticeship that centers on Paris. The young Miró admired Vincent van Gogh, Pablo Picasso, Henri Matisse. His work reflects these enthusiasms. He developed a style more his own, "detailism," which he sometimes related to the art of Japan, that represents familiar objects and people with heightened clarity of detail and precision of line. But "detailism" was not yet a mature style. Miró explained in 1968: "Fauvism and Cubism taught me only severe and formal disciplines. There was a silent revolt inside me. Surrealism allowed me to go beyond formal research; it took me to the heart of poetry, to the heart of joy: the joy of discovering what I am doing after I have done it, of feeling the meaning and the title of a painting grow inside me as I work on it."[4] Miró mentions his affinity for Japanese writing, too. Referring to *Mural Painting for the Cell of a Solitary Man* (1968), one of a triptych of works, each consisting only of a line drawn on a white ground, he says he spent several years practicing the line, only one day to feel "joy": "I picked up my brush and drew the line in a single gesture. But," he adds, "I did not accept it as final until after another month of silence . . ."[5]

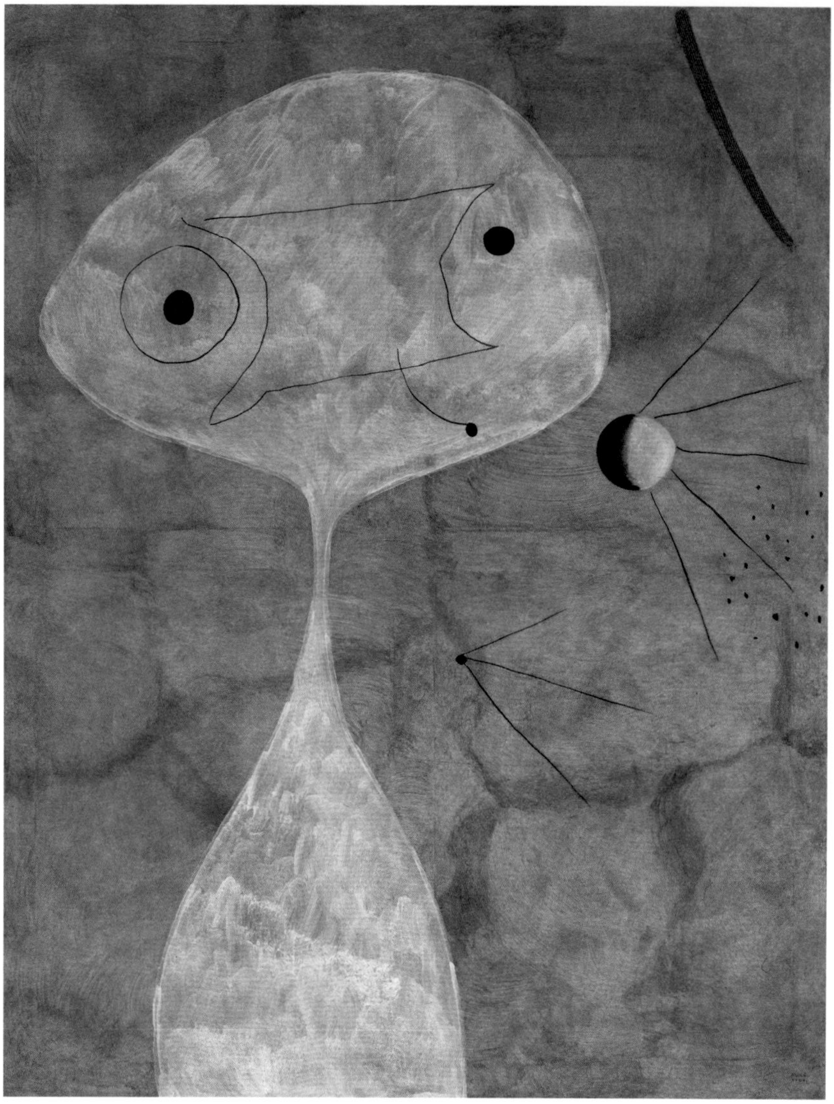

Notice Miró's emphasis on the retrospective contemplation of his line. Accepting it as a success—and therefore, accepting the work as an accomplishment in the art of painting—required looking backward at it. This is a common trope in writing by modernist artists and is key to understanding Miró's later work.

Further, note that Miró's account of his development skips a crucial step. His renunciation of the severe formal disciplines of Fauvism and Cubism predated his contact with official Surrealism. When Denys Chevalier asked him in 1962 about his "assassination of painting," Miró answered that "it came out of Dada and my admiration for Marcel Duchamp," as well as from an "inner protest."[6] These early mature works, including *Pastorale* (1923–24), the "dream paintings" such as *Painting [Man with a Pipe]* (1925; this page), positioned Miró to assume a role in early Surrealism. He left again a few years later, but by that time André Breton could praise Miró's spontaneous creation—his "psychic automatism"—on the strength of paintings that seemed to combine a rare painterly gift with a protean and unexpected world of dream imagery. But Miró's radical combination of open fields of scumbled color (rubbed into the fabric of the canvas) and drawn motifs was really an attack on the art of painting, an attempt to "assassinate painting," in the paintings' extreme bareness, their resistance to traditional notions of space and volume. This turn against painting offers a glimpse of Miró's kinship with Duchamp—even if Duchamp left painting behind and Miró chose to work within it.

Pintura (Hombre con pipa) (Painting [Man with a Pipe])
1925
Oil on canvas
57½ × 44⅞ in. (146 × 114 cm)
Museo Nacional Centro de Arte Reina Sofía, Madrid, Spain

Another crisis closes the 1920s: Miró was drummed out of the Surrealist movement along with a few other dissidents. He turned his back on the metaphorical language of his dream paintings and assumed a new, remarkably aggressive tack toward painting—a willful, almost ugly harshness. As Spain descended with much of Europe into fascism, and war engulfed the environs and companions of his youthful success, Miró's painting expressed more violence and anxiety.

Miró had first entered an American collection in 1927, when Katherine Dreier, undoubtedly under Duchamp's guidance, bought *The Somersault* (1924; p. 42, bottom).[7] Throughout the 1930s, Miró's work found its way into U.S. exhibitions and collections.[8] The Second World War prevented him from visiting the 1941 retrospective of his works at the Museum of Modern Art in New York. This show established Miró's widespread and since-then unwavering popularity in this country. In 1947, Miró traveled to Cincinnati, Ohio, for a mural commission. He met American artists, became the subject of a book by the modernist critic Clement Greenberg, and gave an interview in a short-lived but important journal, *Possibilities*, edited by the painter Robert Motherwell, the critic Harold Rosenberg, and the composer John Cage.[9] The art historian Barbara Rose claims Miró deeply influenced postwar American painting. Offering an alternative to the purity of Piet Mondrian's abstraction—one that permitted subject matter without official Surrealism's dream imagery and facile notion of automatism—Miró's example informed the work of Arshile Gorky, Jackson Pollock, and Motherwell, as well as Hans Hofmann, William Baziotes, David Hare, David Smith, Mark Rothko, Clyfford Still, and Barnett Newman. Indeed, Rose claims that Miró's way of rubbing thinned pigment not just onto, but *into* the support "supplied Greenberg with a rationale to launch a school of 'stain' painters notable for sinking pigment into canvas."[10] Presumably the latter would include Helen Frankenthaler, Morris Louis, and Kenneth Noland.

Miró claimed more than once to have responded to the younger Americans. "I admire very much the energy and vitality of American painters," he told Francis Lee in his *Possibilities* interview. "I especially like their enthusiasm and freshness. This I find inspiring."[11] A few years after his visit to New York, Miró reports having been struck and inspired by a 1952 exhibition of Pollock's work at the Galerie Paul Facchetti in Paris. Speaking of American painting to Margit Rowell, Miró said, "It showed me the liberties we can take, and how far we could go, beyond the limits. In a sense, it freed me."[12] Dripped, drizzled and splashed paint, handprints, and large canvases of open color seem to bear out the suggestion of influence.[13] Still, Miró's speaks of *liberty* and not external influence—not of new ideas, but of new access to his own impulses.

Miró's approach to materials and technique had always been free, even aggressive: "to assassinate painting."[14] Although Miró never explained the remark, Anne Umland has described a career of iconoclastic self-reinvention—a determination to question his own art that seems destructive. Some of this aggression takes the form of a primitivism that drew Miró to cave painting. "My favorite schools of painting are as far back as possible," he told Francis Lee, "the cave painters—the [Italian] primitives."[15] To take seriously Miró's desire to go "as far back as possible," means situating his sensibility at the threshold of art, at its origins in marking. At that notional point, graffiti and stains could be seen as such, and not already as art.[16]

We are left with a dilemma, then: Do we see in Miró's ongoing attack on painting—in his turn to handprints and stains in his work of the sixties and seventies—a return to the prehistory of art, the caves of Altamira and Lascaux, or a projection forward toward high modernism, to the drips and handprints of Pollock and the stain paintings of Frankenthaler, Louis, and Noland? In light of modernism's dual embrace of new frontiers and primordial roots, let's seek Miró's own entry into that paradox, his sense of his relationship to history.

Miró himself placed his initiation into modernism's conflicted logic in his youthful interest in Dada. Remember, though, that unlike Duchamp, Miró did not leave painting: "What can I say," he told Denys Chevalier, "I can't be anything other than a painter. Every challenge to painting is a paradox—from the moment that challenge is expressed in a work."[17]

MIRÓ'S STRATEGY

Miró's strategy was different from Duchamp's. Duchamp staged a contest between aesthetic and institutional legitimation, which implicated historical institutions and questioned criteria of judgment. Miró seems to have staged a parallel gambit. In it, he pitted the work's claim to represent an absent world vividly—to give it *presence*—against the work of art as an artifact of (or a moment in) the history of style. The work was to *overcome*, by the intensity of this effect of presence, the very real sense in which it was an element in the historical series that constitutes the history of painting, or indeed, that constitutes Miró's own career, understood as a development or succession of styles or an ongoing attempt to "assassinate painting." This is what it means to say that Miró's work needs to be understood in its relation to the history of modern art if we are to understand it as art at all.

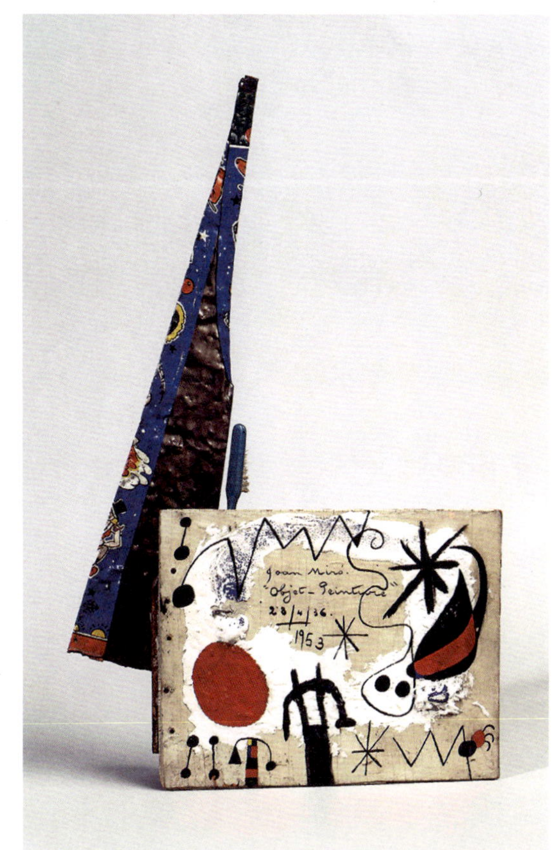

Objet-peinture (Painting Object)
1936/1953
Painted iron sheet, clothespin, toothbrush, paint, wood, plywood, and whistle
17⅜ x 11⅛ x 3⅜ in.
(44 x 28.2 x 8.5 cm)
Museo Nacional Centro de Arte Reina Sofía, Madrid, Spain

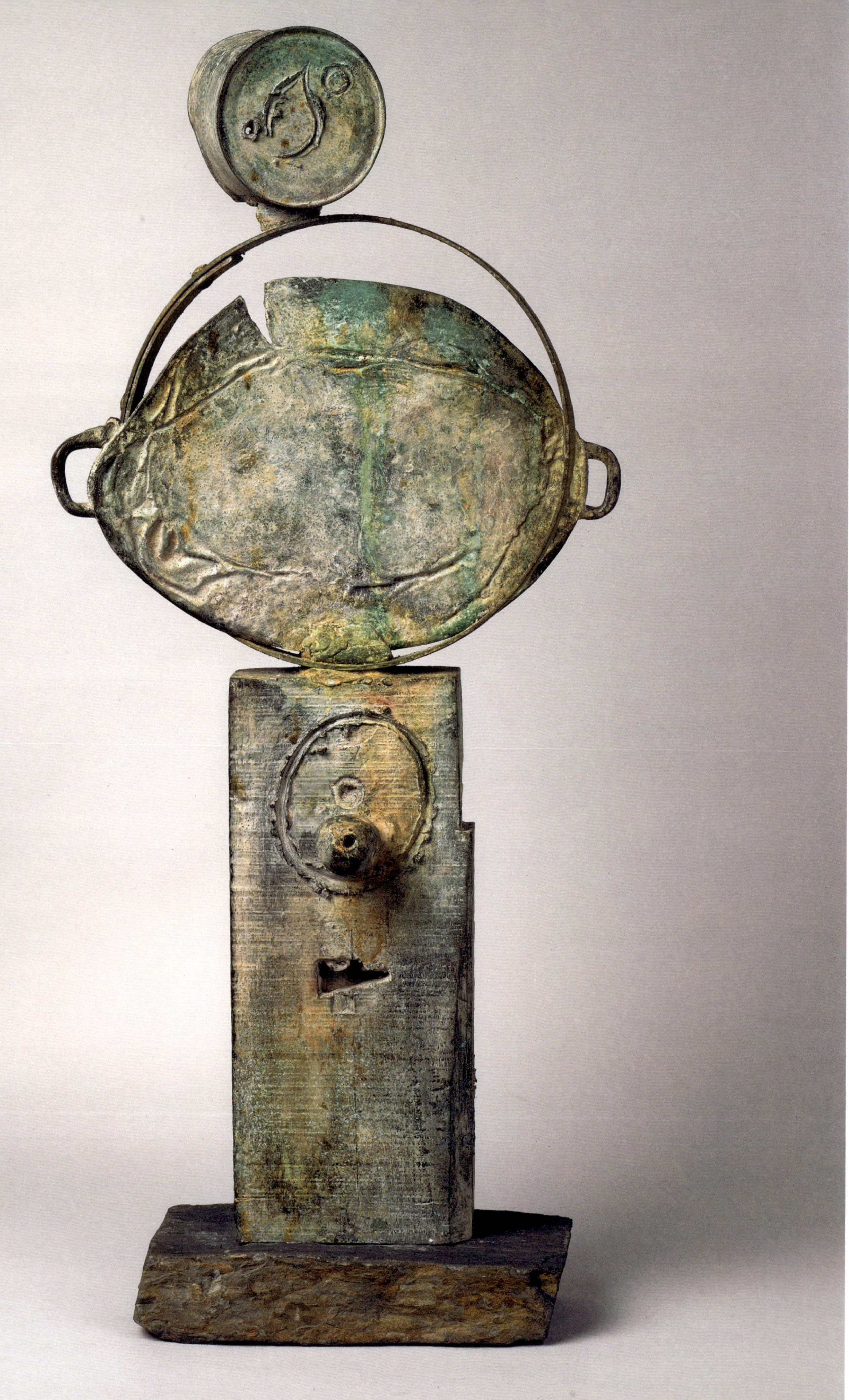

First, let's try to understand Miró's attempt to bring presence and absence together in the work of art. In 1924 Miró wrote to a close friend of his, the writer Michel Leiris, about one of his current projects, *Portrait of Miss K* (1924; this page):

> *Figuration of one of my latest x's (I can't find the word for it here; don't want to say either canvas or painting). Portrait of a charming lady friend from Paris—I begin with the idea of touching her body* very chastely, *beginning with her side and going up to her head. Profile drawn in charcoal.*[18]

Already, Miró has made all the key points. Miró was writing from Mont-roig, in the Spanish province of Tarragona, so his recourse to a sitter in Paris bears out his general preference for motifs at some significant distance, in geography and memory. Yet he collapses those distances by imagining (or recalling) *touching her*, then reverting immediately to his own procedures in mark-making: "profile drawn in charcoal." Miró implies an analogy—almost an *identity*—between his caress and the action of drawing. That imagined near-identity between the caress and the gesture with charcoal allows the image to be an "x," neither a "canvas or painting." This is Miró's attack on painting, at least as it stood in summer 1924.[19]

Let's suppose that Miró aimed (in 1924) to revitalize painting by forgetting painting, by displacing the actions, even as he performed them, onto imagined or recollected actions in the absent world of the subject of his painting. He refused attention to the "x" as a new entry in the history of painting, thinking of it as a reenacted caress instead, precisely in order to secure for it—to paraphrase Duchamp: like a comet with its tail in front—a place for it in the history of painting.[20] Or to put it in Miró's own words: "Every challenge to painting is a paradox—from the moment that challenge is expressed in a work."[21]

Thirty years later, Miró turned his hand again to projects (literally: things thrown forward) from the twenties and thirties. The earliest one I know is a construction from 1953 that is literally built outward from a small painting of 1936, *Objet-peinture* (1936/1953; p. 57). It is a small painted wooden panel from the thirties to which Miró added a toothbrush, a piece of metal hardware, some painting on the panel's reverse, and a slice of pressed metal bearing the image of dancers, which is supported by a clothespin and held forward—projected—from the surface of the painting into the beholder's space.

Compare the "legs" of the clothespin to the legs of the dancers in the image on metal—almost like the comparison of caressing a woman with drawing her contour, only now with a more literal, material quality. It's not just the formal similarity between the clothespin's members and the dancers'; it's the differences in levels of fictionality, of scale, and of material presence that count. Considering this juxtaposition in relation to the painting that offers its support, things become more complex still. The forms of the 1953 dancers seem to step brightly into our space while they echo the 1936 painting behind them, offered to us, like Duchamp's gaudy necktie, to embody, to show us, their relation to an older work. And the relation is something like this: the past (1936) is representation; the present (1953) is a readymade and obdurately material. A commonplace artifact enters into the work of art via the relationship constructed for it to more traditional work, work that has earned the artworld's imprimatur. Perhaps one can feel that the objects of the here and now take on a new meaning if they can be thought of as the realizations of representations—dreams or memories—of long ago. The painted panel, coming before years of war, must have seemed to have come from another life.

Personnage (Figure)
1970
Patinated bronze
30⅛ x 14 x 6⅛ in.
(76.5 x 35.5 x 15.5 cm)

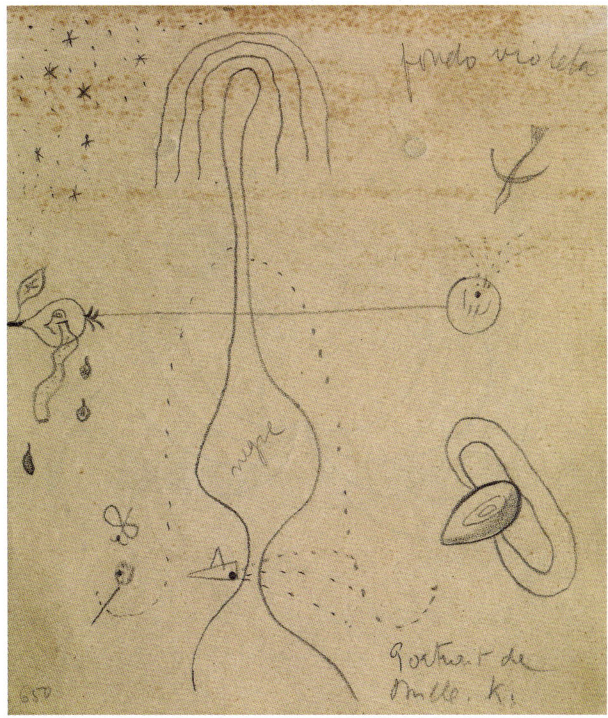

Portrait de Mlle K
(Portrait of Miss K
[Preliminary drawing
for *Portrait of Mrs. K*]*)*
1924
Graphite pencil on paper
7½ x 6½ in. (19.1 x 16.5 cm)
Fundació Joan Miró,
Barcelona

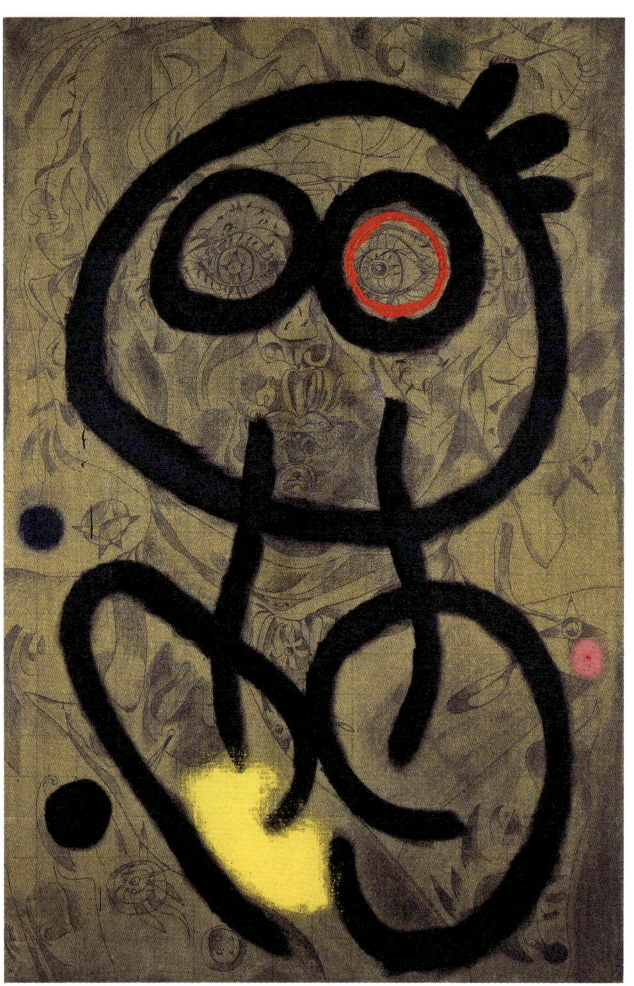

Autoportrait (Self-Portrait)
1937–38/1960
Oil and pencil on canvas
57½ × 38³⁄₁₆ in. (146 × 97 cm)
Collection Emili Fernández Miró. On permanent loan to the Fundació Joan Miró, Barcelona

Now let's consider the sculptures Miró began to make, first sporadically in the forties and mid fifties, and then in earnest from the mid sixties on. Some of the examples in the present exhibition forcefully reveal the deep similarity of Miró's sculpture to the 1936/53 object. A bronze sculpture, *Woman in the Night* (1967; p. 21), rises from its base like a thin slab. On the face is a linear shape filled with linear elements that evoke hair. I feel confident in identifying this with the woman of the title. On the reverse is a star—or the set of crossing lines that Miró uses for such celestial bodies. Rather than depict the woman as a form set against the night sky (you can't see the figure of the woman and the star simultaneously), Miró has used this slablike form to unite in its thickness the form of the figure with the space of the night sky. It represents something like their continuity with one another and an absolute separation between them, like the separation between two sides of a wall.

A 1970 sculpture, *Woman and Bird* (p. 74), shows a similar star shape on the reverse of a torso cast from a planar metal object. The front of that element bears an X shape—evidently part of the original found object—that I am tempted to think of as echoed in the handwrought asterisk on the back. Again, the thickness of the cast plate unites the graphic elements on its front and back. And again, they can be aligned with the body of the figure and with the heavenly array of stars. But the body of the sculpture also unites the found and the handmade—the crossed lines Miró discovers and the asterisk he draws. Perhaps this could be understood as Dupin and Suquet understand Duchamp's necktie in the *Large Glass*, as uniting the figure with the celestial space of the Bride's register.

In another work, *Figure* (1970; p. 58), the figure incorporates a frame-like motif (perhaps a hoop for stretching a needlepoint canvas—which would make an ironic, self-reflexive point about the pictorial quality of the sculpture's space[22]), which frames an element cast from a folded basket. The framing device evokes the deep space of painting or the contour of the head. Whether you see it as a frame through which to look or as a hat, say, or as an echo of the basket-form that seems to be the head, the collapsed basket serves the same function as the slab uniting and dividing the woman and the night did: its bronze-cast body is both the two sides and their union, an evocation of the open space of the basket and the reduction of it to (another) slab, a thickness. Other sculptures use similar techniques to draw attention to their thicknesses: a *Figure* of 1981 (p. 63) appears to be cast from a folded expanse of heavy cloth, perhaps a blanket.

Young Girl (1967; p. 10) places the figure's features along the edges of a frame that can also be understood either as the figure's legs framing the space between them or as the contour of the figure's body, which would be defined by that border and identical with the void it frames. The ambiguity about how to read the framed rectangular space once again draws on the vocabulary of painting (frames and outlines, vistas and contours), only to leave us in doubt about whether we are looking at a figure's body or into heavenly space. *Head in the Night* (1968; p. 65) makes the theme of the frame-within-the-figure still plainer. A rectangular frame, almost complete, is attached to the circular head. An oval handle projects from the top and bottom edges of the frame, breaking the frontal plane to enclose the sculpture in three-dimensional space. Whether that space is to be thought of as the volume of the figure's head or as an envelope of deep space around the figure's head is unclear. That very ambiguity restates the theme: in his sculptures, Miró unites the figure and deep space ("*Head in the* Night").

RETURNING TO RETROSPECTIVE TEMPORALITY

Poème à la gloire des étincelles (Poem to the Glory of Sparkles)
1969
Acrylic on canvas
51³⁄₁₆ × 76¾ in. (130 × 195 cm)

Detail on following page.

Let's get back to the retrospective nature of Miró's later sculptures. You can see it in the appropriation of traditional objects, evocative of old-fashioned home life, as if they were suited to represent the peasant personages of Miró's imaginary world by their metonymic connection to its people. An old basket or fork or shards of traditional pottery, a long wooden spoon for stirring a rustic meal,[23] or a grill, like the one the peasant in *The Hunter (Catalan Landscape)* (1923–24; p. 43, bottom) or one of Miró's other early paintings uses to prepare a meal in the field: these are the materials of which these personages are cast. Perhaps one might see in them something of the Duchampian readymade; or, at the very least, something in the spirit of Dada.[24] The found imagery also recalls Miró's precursors in modernist sculpture, such as Picasso and Julio González, whom Miró mentions in some working notes.[25] In all these ways, the works convey the presence and the absence of another time and place.[26]

Miró paintings also incorporate the passage of time and earlier moments in his career. The best known of these is a self-portrait from 1960, *Self-Portrait II* (1937–38/1960; p. 60), executed on a copy Miró commissioned of a self-portrait drawing with oil from 1937–38. This unfinished work, *Self-Portrait I*, serves as the premise enacted in the 1960 revision. The later work is not a reworking of the older self-portrait; rather, the two self-portrait images are distinct, one superimposed on the other. The delay in time is not a failure of the work, but an integral feature of its conception.

Dupin calls the painted image from 1960 "a violent and ironic obliteration of the previous work." He calls the heavy painted marks "graffiti," a kind of defacement. "It is as though Miró's face were trying to hide, but not to disappear, behind a Mironian personage."[27] This leads him to a conclusion about the place of such a mask in Miró's aesthetic: "The image of the artist's liberated subjectivity withdraws behind the grid of his creations, behind the screen of a work whose proudest ambition is to be anonymous. 'A profoundly individualistic gesture is anonymous. By being anonymous, it can

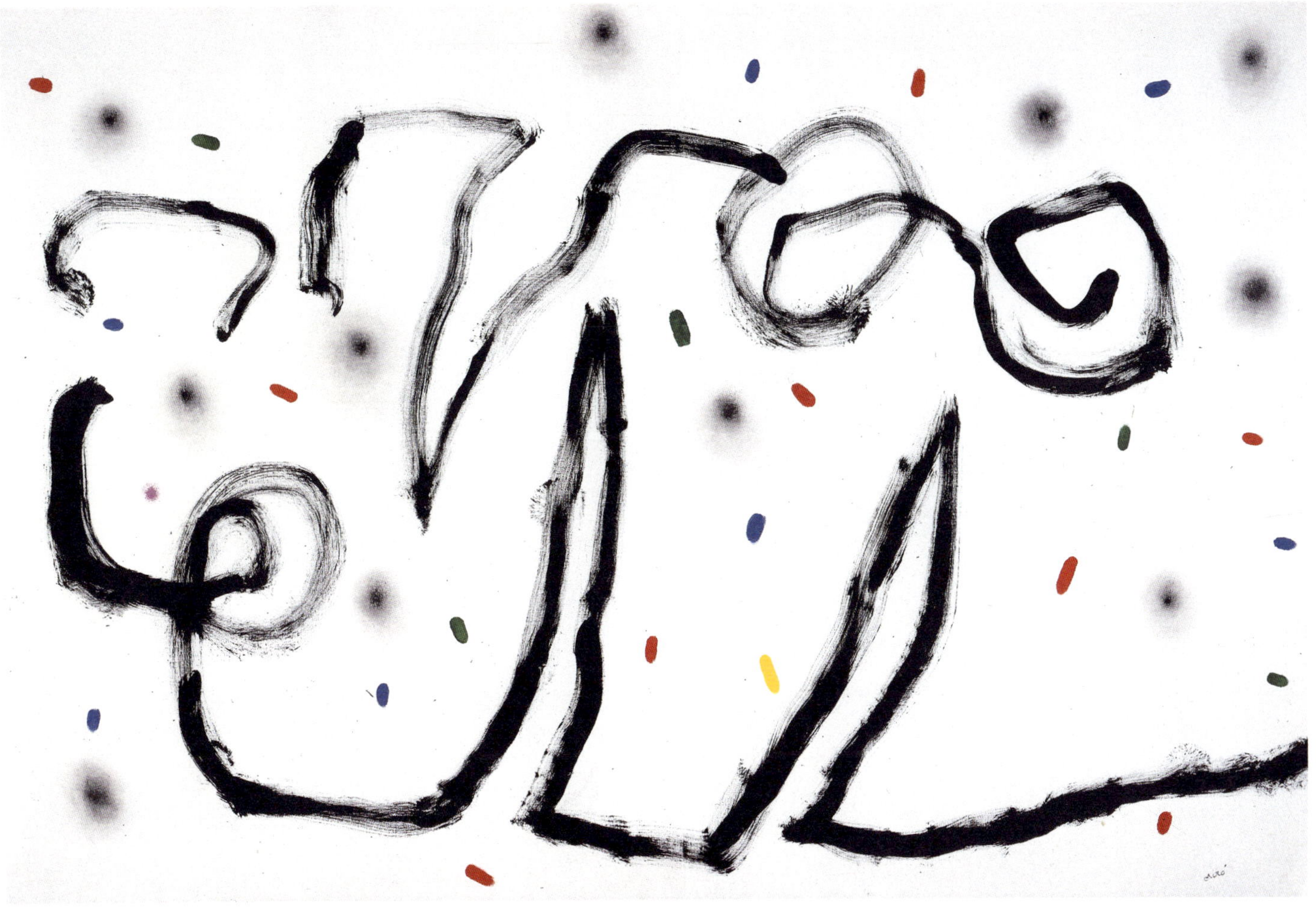

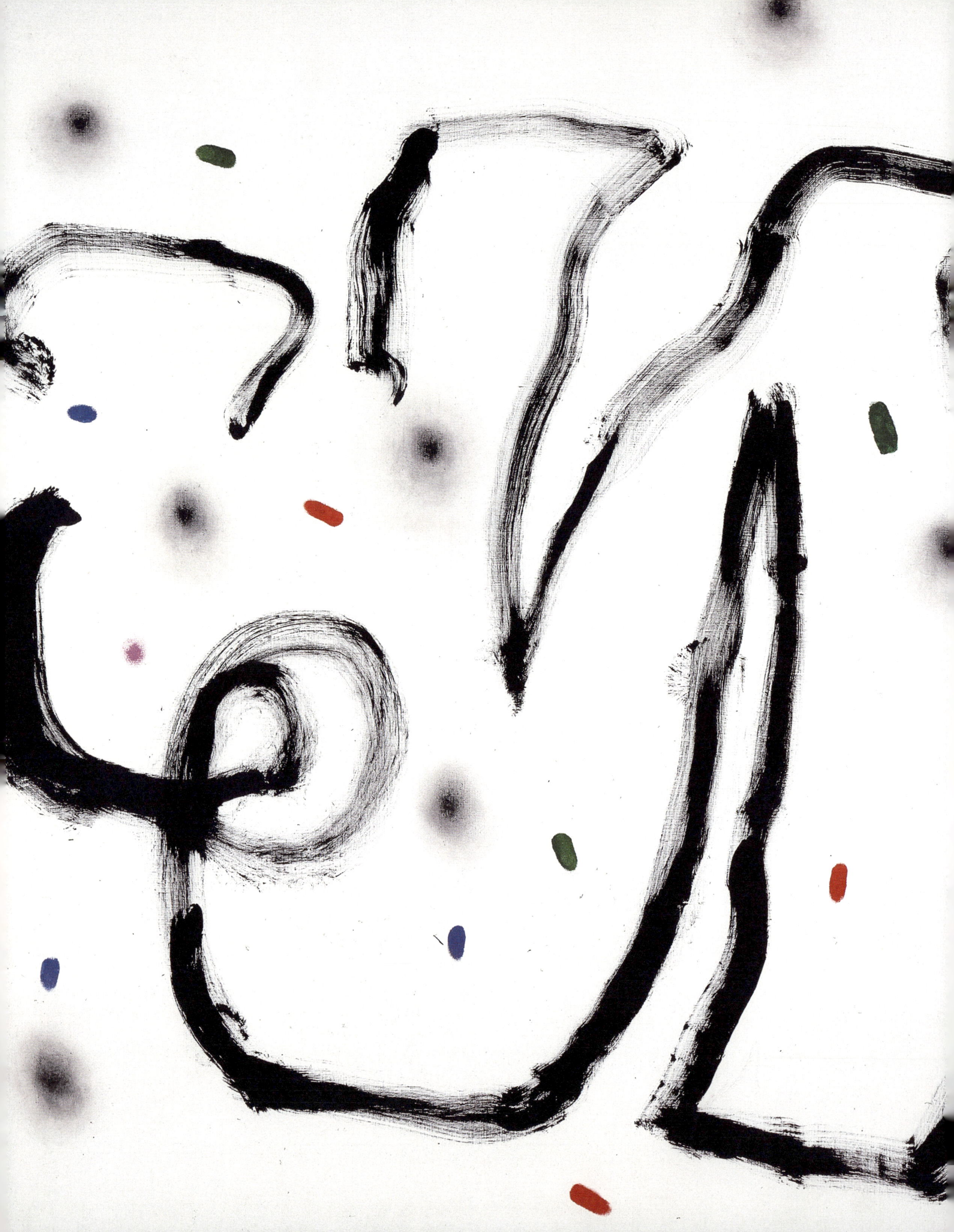

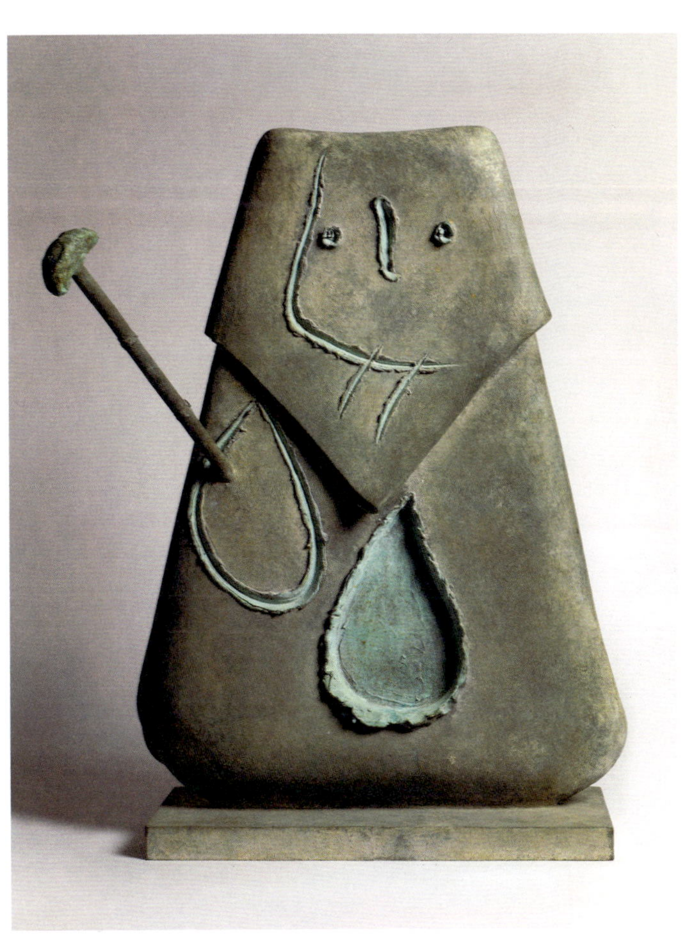

Personnage (Figure), 1981, patinated bronze, 35 1/16 × 25 9/16 × 17 15/16 in. (89 × 65 × 44 cm), front. Back view below.

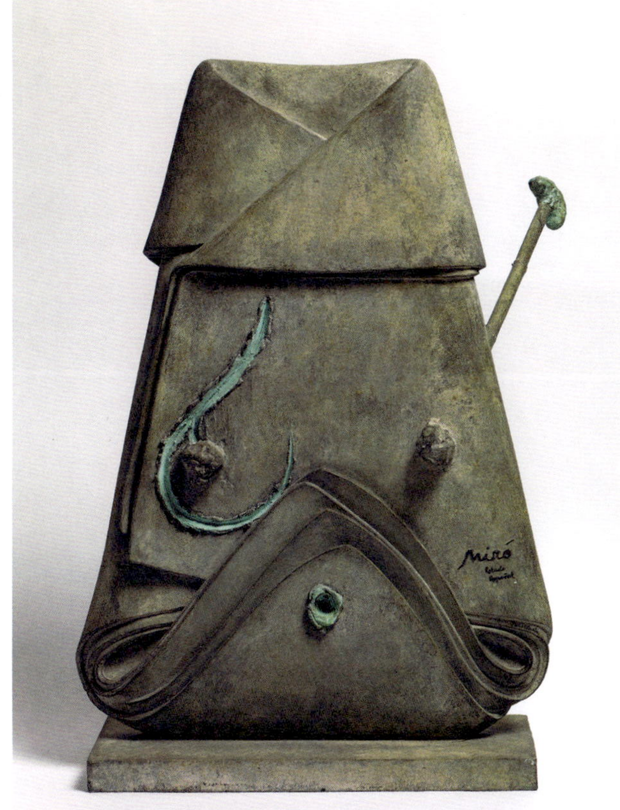

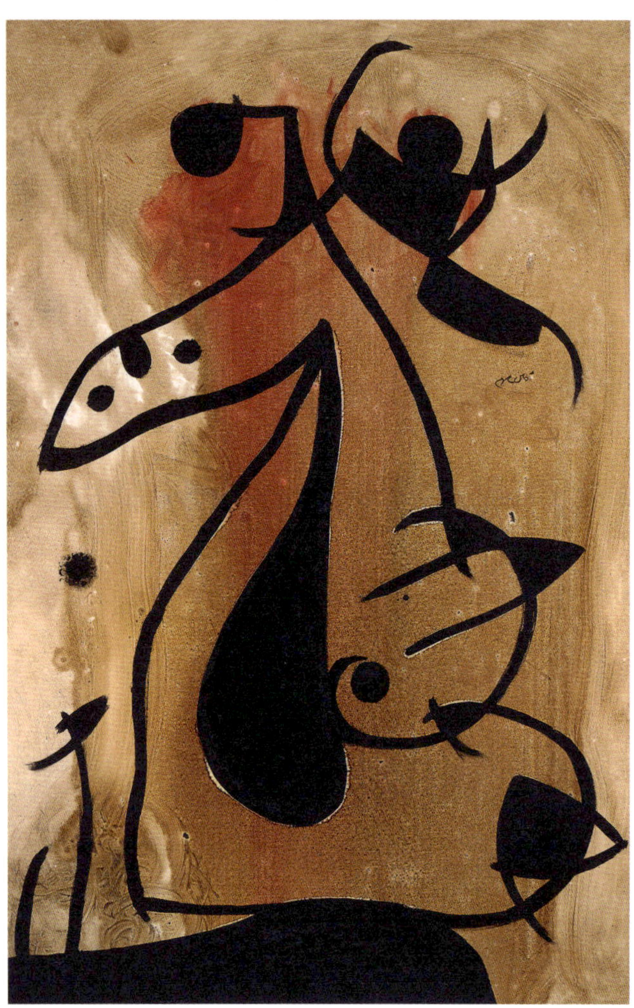

Femme oiseau I (Bird Woman I)
1977
Oil on canvas
76¾ × 51³⁄₁₆ in. (195 × 130 cm)

attain universality.'"[28] Again, then, we have the notion of an artist's personality merging with a kind of mark-making that recedes to the threshold of history—graffiti or cave painting—and thereby becomes universal, transcending the institutions that the avant-garde seeks to discredit and escape.

In the mid fifties, Miró moved into a new studio on Mallorca designed by his old friend Josep Lluís Sert just above the beach at Cala Mayor. There he lived out the decades of Francisco Franco's dictatorship in relative obscurity and safety. Miró found himself unpacking, and thus confronting, years of mothballed work. Thereafter, Miró occasionally incorporated an older work into a newer one—as in the 1936/1953 assemblage and the 1960 self-portrait. But he found ways to introduce history's thickness into a single session of work, too.

Consider a representative work in the present exhibition, *Poem to the Glory of Sparkles* (1969; p. 61), which uses an array of points to represent celestial distance. The "sparkles" of the title suggest twinkling stars or shimmering fireworks. The reference to a poem evokes Miró's old use of calligraphy to describe close attention to small, linear motifs[29] and the painting-poems of the later 1920s. A closer look at the canvas shows that some of the dots are scumbled, while others are thick paint on the surface. (A pair in the lower left makes the comparison neatly, a black scumbled dot and a thick blue one.)

By scumbling color and sandpapering patches of color, Miró, Dupin says, makes his colors:

> *seem to well up from the canvas, at the same time bringing out the latter's texture and weave; one would swear this union had been the work of weathering, rather than of human hands. It is the memory of the walls of a prehistoric cavern that is restored to us in all its freshness, as though the signs and forms came to be inscribed, and the colors to sing the very substance of time.*[30]

Thus the canvas's history is telescoped to the impersonal and slower tempo of weather and of human history, drawing the threshold of culture to the present.

This presence of a kind of temporality in the fabric and layers of Miró's painting is to be seen everywhere. In *Bird Woman I* (1977; this page) a thin, painterly background evokes both a dense atmosphere and, in the patterns of brushwork, drawing. Look at the sweeping gestural archway at left, right, and top, or the red graphisms underneath the upper members of the black figure. That phantom drawing, which exists as part of the atmosphere in which it floats yet also seems to anticipate the black lines that define the figure, suggests some sort of agency, some draftsman as impersonal and elusive as the phantom forms in the thin paint. The heavier black lines—especially the couple of circular nodes in the upper left-hand corner of the painting—trace the edges of the red gestural marks and may even seem to occupy spaces defined for them, as if in response to the earlier red paint. Whether or not you accept precisely that description of the relation, what matters is the impression one gets that the red drawing comes first and in some way affects the black forms of the Bird Woman. One might similarly argue that the archway traced in the thin background makes the framing shape of the painting into a represented space in the picture, a represented place.[31]

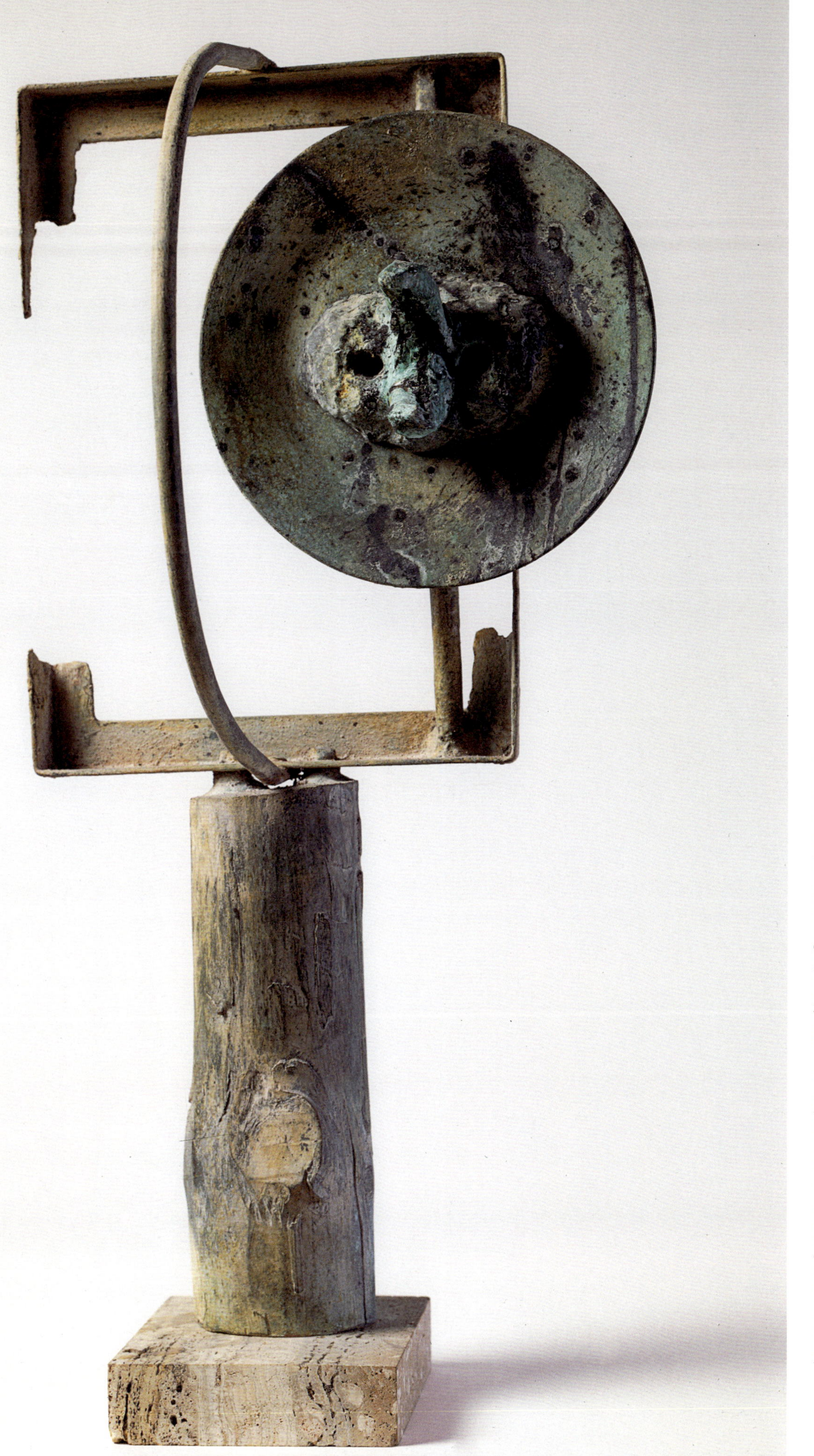

Tête dans la nuit (Head in the Night), 1968, patinated bronze, 28 1/8 × 14 3/16 × 12 3/16 in. (71.5 × 36 × 31 cm)

In *Bird in Space* (1976; pp. 81–83), a blue dot, a red dot, and a long arrow broken by staccato bursts of ellipsis points float in a field of white brushstrokes, barely discernable against the white background. One is tempted, in front of the painting, to bring the lively field of white brushstrokes into play, pictorially. Here, they appear to converge on the blue dot; there, they follow the winding arrow like a current of air. If they are the space through which the bird flies, and the arrow is bird and its course, then the field of white brushstrokes are also the currents that toss the bird as it goes. Seen this way, the picture recalls an important work of the twenties, *Un Oiseau poursuit une abeille et la baisse* (1926–27; opposite page), in which a long, gestural curve defines the path of a bird as it chases a bee. Perhaps letting *Bird in Space* remind us of the earlier work is yet another way of letting the past determine the course of the later work, maybe even in something like the way the gestural white underpainting influences the flight of the bird.

A very last painting offers a final opportunity for reflection on these themes. *Women VI* (1969; p. 29) evidences Miró's characteristic techniques: the scumbling and the canvas's weave, the small points that evoke the celestial remoteness, the heavily retraced paint—often clearly applied via the physical intimacy of fingerpainting. The thickness of the paint separates and joins the infinite distance, and the fingertip range of the figures should be familiar by now—from the slabs and the frame-figures of the sculptures, from Duchamp's necktie connecting the bachelors to the bride's sky. Take a very close look at the canvas to see something even more striking. Some drawing on the bare canvas—maybe clearest in the upper right-hand quadrant—is reminiscent of certain works of the early to mid twenties, such as *Catalan Landscape* (1923–24; p. 43, bottom), *Pastorale* (1923–24), and *The Somersault* (1924; p. 42, bottom), which Duchamp's protégée Katherine Dreier bought in 1927. It may well be that, in his Sert studio, surrounded by works he'd unpacked, Miró attempted one more experiment in retrospective temporality, letting not the caves but his own prehistory shine out of the weave of the canvas to oppose its remoteness to his women's physical presence.

ACKNOWLEDGMENTS

I would like to thank Kimerly Rorschach, Chiyo Ishikawa, Catharina Manchanda, and Zora Hutlova Foy of the Seattle Art Museum for offering me the occasion to think about Miró's later work; Carmen Fernández Aparicio, Paloma Calopa, Carmen Muro, and a team of preparators at the Museo Nacional Centro de Arte Reina Sofía for their expertise and assistance before, during, and after my visit to the museum; Dean Lu Ann Homza of the College of William and Mary for making it possible for me to conduct research in Spain; the conservators Kay Krueger of the National Gallery of Art and Suzanne Penn of the Philadelphia Museum of Art, who shared their wisdom with me; Michael Schreyach of Trinity University in San Antonio and Todd Cronan of Emory University, Atlanta, who read and discussed; and Beth Chapple, for very fast and intense copyediting.

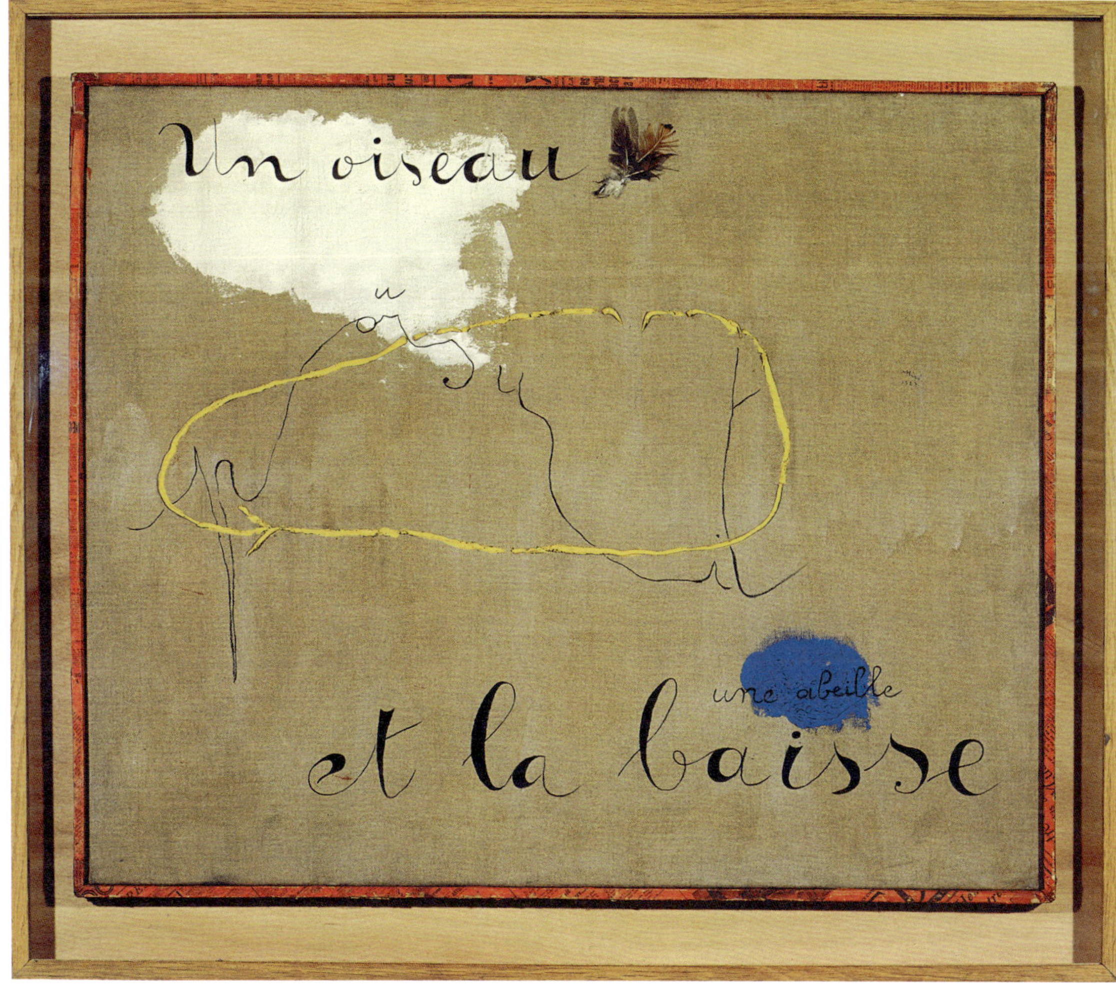

Un Oiseau poursuit une abeille et la baisse (Painting Poem [A Bird Pursuing a Bee])
1926–27
Oil, aqueous medium, and feathers on glue-sized canvas
31⅞ x 39⅜ in. (81 × 100 cm)
Private Collection

NOTES

1. Jacques Dupin and Jean Suquet, "Un livre naufragé . . ." in Marcel Duchamp and Joan Miró, *Demande d'emploi*, intro. Jacques Dupin and Jean Suquet (Paris: L'Échoppe, 2002), 49–54. The quotation appears on page 54 and in the illustration on page 55: "une sorte de forme principe sur laquelle le tableau en entire repose."

2. Ibid., 54.

3. Ibid.

4. Miró, in Pierre Bourcier, "Article (excerpts)" in *Joan Miró: Selected Writings and Interviews*, 275; originally published as "Miró au Coeur de la joie," *Les Nouvelles Littéraires* (August 8, 1968).

5. Margit Rowell, ed., *Joan Miró: Selected Writings and Interviews*, trans. Paul Auster and Patricia Mathews (New York: Da Capo, 1992): 275.

6. Denys Chevalier, "Miró" in Rowell, *Joan Miró: Selected Writings*, 266; originally published in *Aujourd'hui: Art et Architecture* (November 1962).

7. Barbara Rose, *Miró in America*, with essays by Judith McCandless and Duncan MacMillan (The Museum of Fine Arts, Houston, April 21–June 27, 1982), 15. Exhibition catalog.

8. Barbara Rose, "Miró in America" in Rose, *Miró in America*, 6.

9. Clement Greenberg, *Miró* (New York: Quadrangle Press, 1948) and *Possibilities* 1 (Winter 1947/1948).

10. Rose, *Miró in America*, 28.

11. Francis Lee, "Interview with Miró" in Rowell, ed., *Joan Miró: Selected Writings*, 204; originally published in *Possibilities* 1.

12. Margit Rowell, "Bleu II, 1961, de Joan Miró," *Cahiers du Musée d'Art Moderne* (1984), 58; cited in Jacques Dupin, *Miró* (Paris: Flammarion, 2004), 303.

13. For instances of such suggestions, see Rosalind Krauss's and Margit Rowell's essays in *Joan Miró: Magnetic Fields* (Solomon R. Guggenheim Museum, New York, 1972 [Exhibition catalog]), 37, 64, and then 65 and 143 for important qualifiers.

14. This is the central theme of Anne Umland, *Joan Miró: Painting and Anti-Painting, 1927–1937*, with Jim Coddington, Robert Lubar, Jordana Mendelson, and Adele Nelson (The Museum of Modern Art, New York, November 2, 2008–January 12, 2009 [Exhibition catalog]).

15. Rowell, *Joan Miró: Selected Writings*, 203.

16. As Rosalind Krauss herself pointed out some years after her suggestion that Miró's painting shared some of the spirit of American color-field painting, that comparison risks mistaking something fundamental about Miró's paintings of the mid twenties and in the critical period around 1930, during which he was close to the circle around Georges Bataille and the journal *Documents*. Rather, she proposes "making them appear not so much as stain paintings, but as stains pure and simple, not so much ideograms as graffiti, not so much dreams as the aggression Miró himself claimed for them at the time" (Krauss, "'Michel, Bataille et moi,'" *October*, vol. 68 [Spring 1994], 25).

17. Rowell, *Joan Miró: Selected Writings*, 266.

18. Ibid., 86.

19. For a fuller discussion of this letter and the drawing to which it evidently refers, see my *Fixed Ecstasy: Joan Miró in the 1920s*, Refiguring Modernism Series (University Park: Pennsylvania State University Press, 2008), 82–85.

20. This phrase, and my remarks about Duchamp throughout this essay, come directly from Thierry de Duve, *Kant after Duchamp* (Cambridge, Mass.: MIT Press, 1996), 141.

21. Rowell, *Joan Miró: Selected Writings*, 266.

22. I would like to thank Carmen Fernández Aparicio for this suggestion.

23. My thanks again to Carmen Fernández Aparicio for this identification.

24. Umland, *Joan Miró*, 44.

25. Rowell, *Joan Miró: Selected Writings*, 175.

26. See my argument about those early paintings in Palermo, *Fixed Ecstasy*, 45–59.

27. Ibid.

28. Ibid. The quotation is from Joan Miró, "I Work Like a Gardener" interview by Yvon Taillandier, 15 February 1959, in Rowell, *Joan Miró: Selected Writings*, 252; originally published as "Miró: je travaille comme un jardinière," *XXe Siècle* (February 15, 1959), 4–5.

29. Palermo, *Fixed Ecstasy*, 17–24.

30. Dupin, *Miró*, 284.

31. In this, it makes me think of Jackson Pollock's work in yet another way. See Michael Schreyach's discussion of "format" in his "Pollock's Formalist Spaces," *nonsite.org* 7 (Fall 2012), http://nonsite.org/article/pollocks-formalist-spaces#foot_src_22_4529.

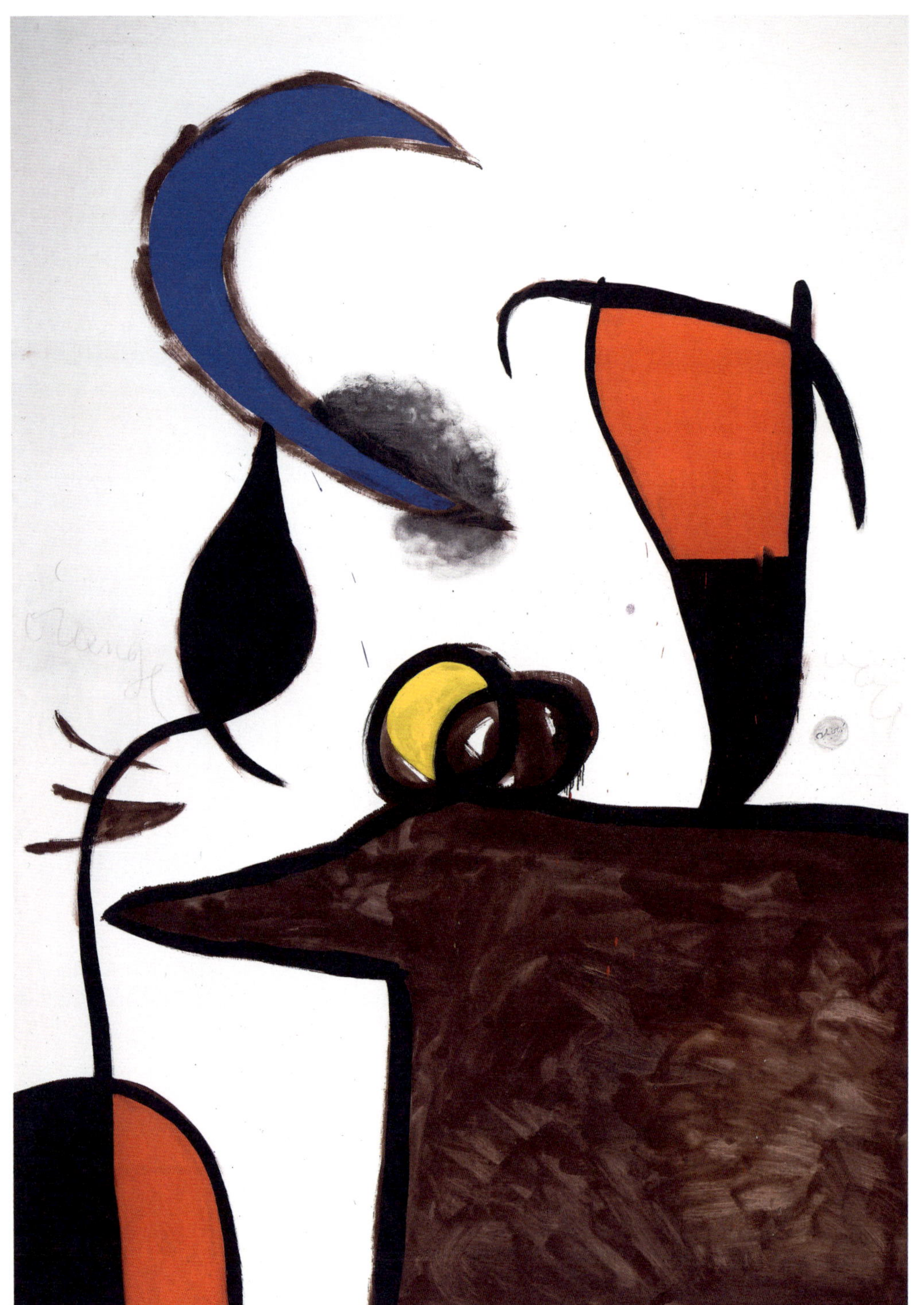

Femmes, oiseau dans la nuit (Women and Bird in the Night), 1974, oil, acrylic, and charcoal pencil on canvas, 102⅜ × 72¹³⁄₁₆ in. (260 × 185 cm)

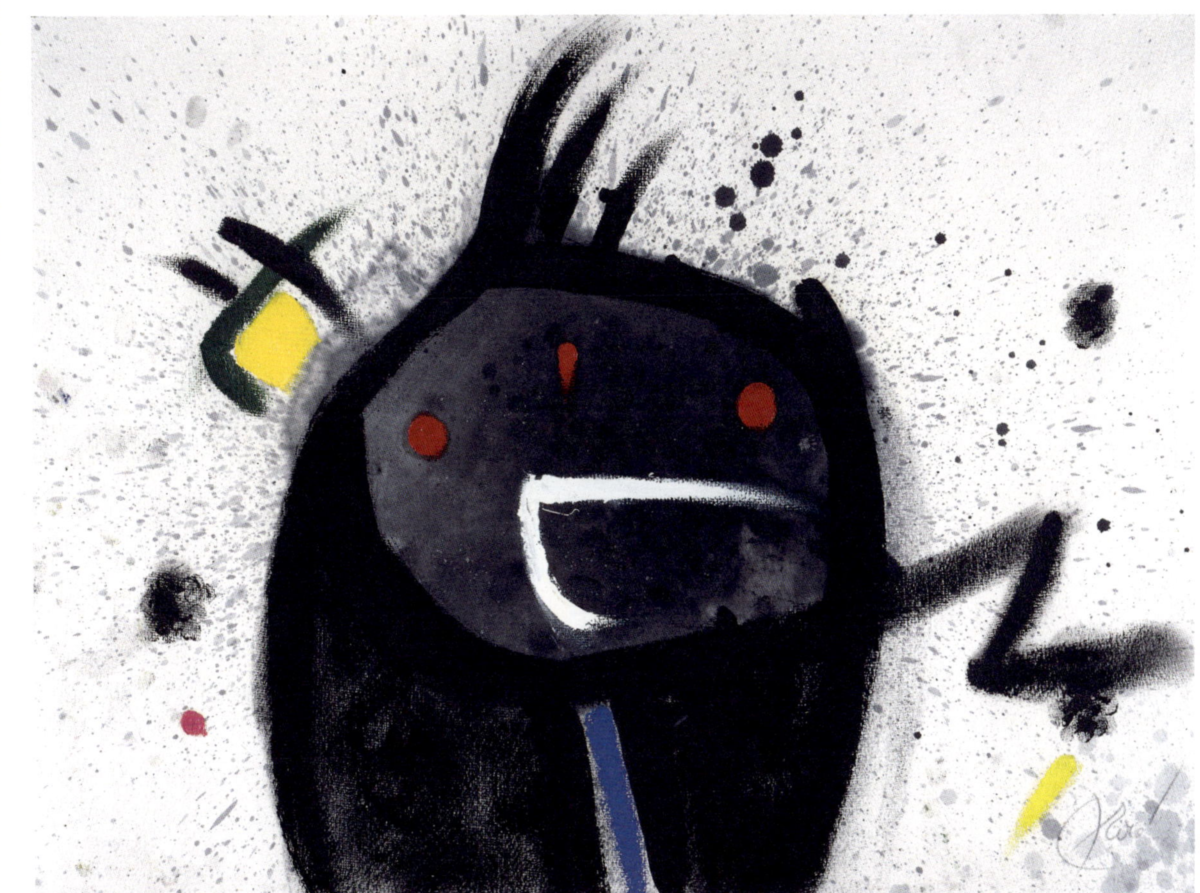

Tête, oiseau (Head, Bird), 1977, lithographic ink and acrylic on Barker paper, 22⅝ × 30¹¹⁄₁₆ in. (57.5 × 78 cm)

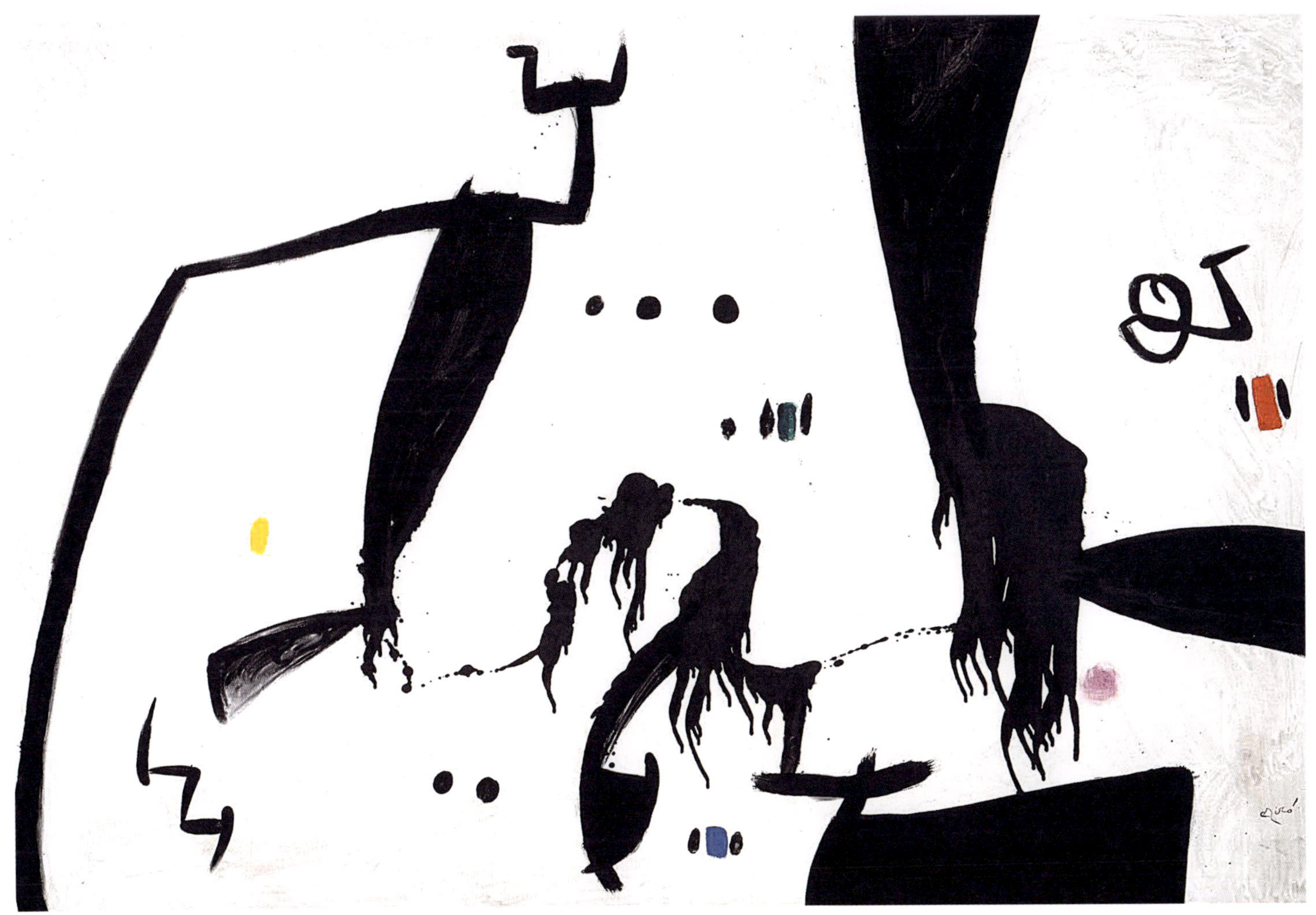

Personnages, oiseaux, constellations (Figures, Birds, Constellations), 1976, oil on canvas, 51 × 76 9/16 in. (129.5 × 194.5 cm)

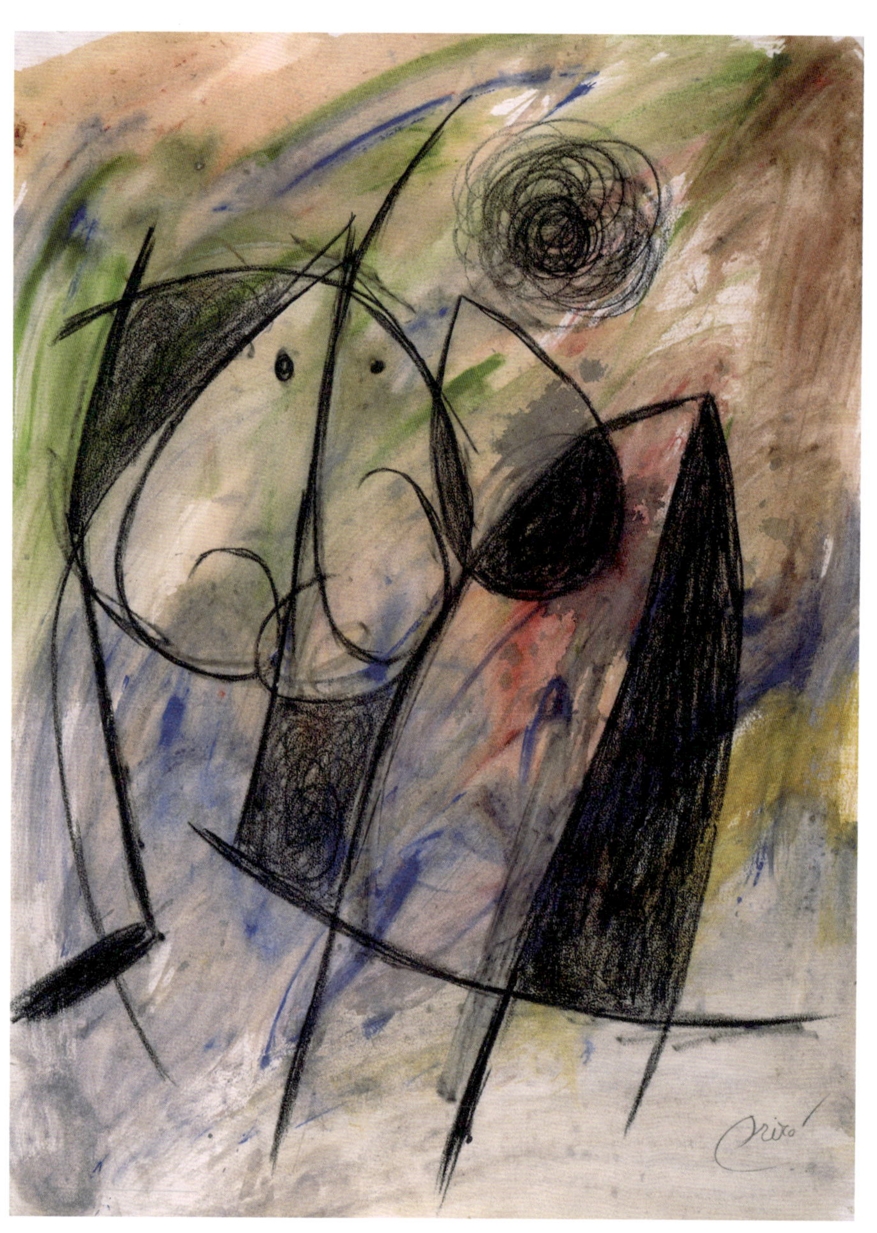

Personnage (Figure), 1977, gouache, wash, and grease pencil on textured Arches paper, 30⅛ × 22 7/16 in. (76.5 × 57 cm)

Danseuse (Dancer), 1981, patinated bronze, 39 15/16 × 22 7/16 × 10 13/16 in. (101.5 × 57 × 27.5 cm)

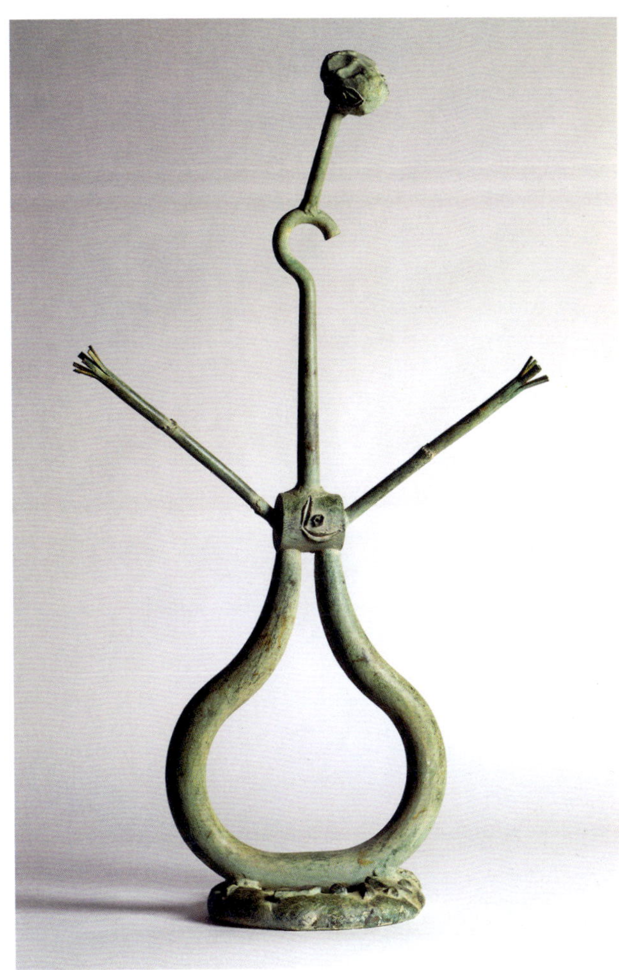

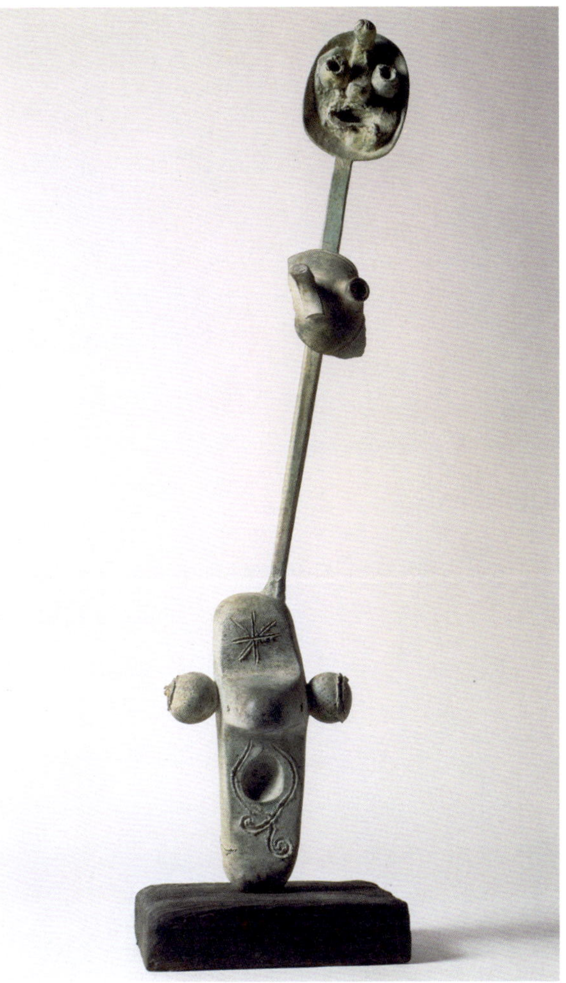

Jeune fille rêvant de l'évasion (Young Woman Dreaming of Evasion), 1969, patinated bronze, 39 × 8 7/8 × 6 7/8 in. (99 × 22.5 × 17.5 cm)

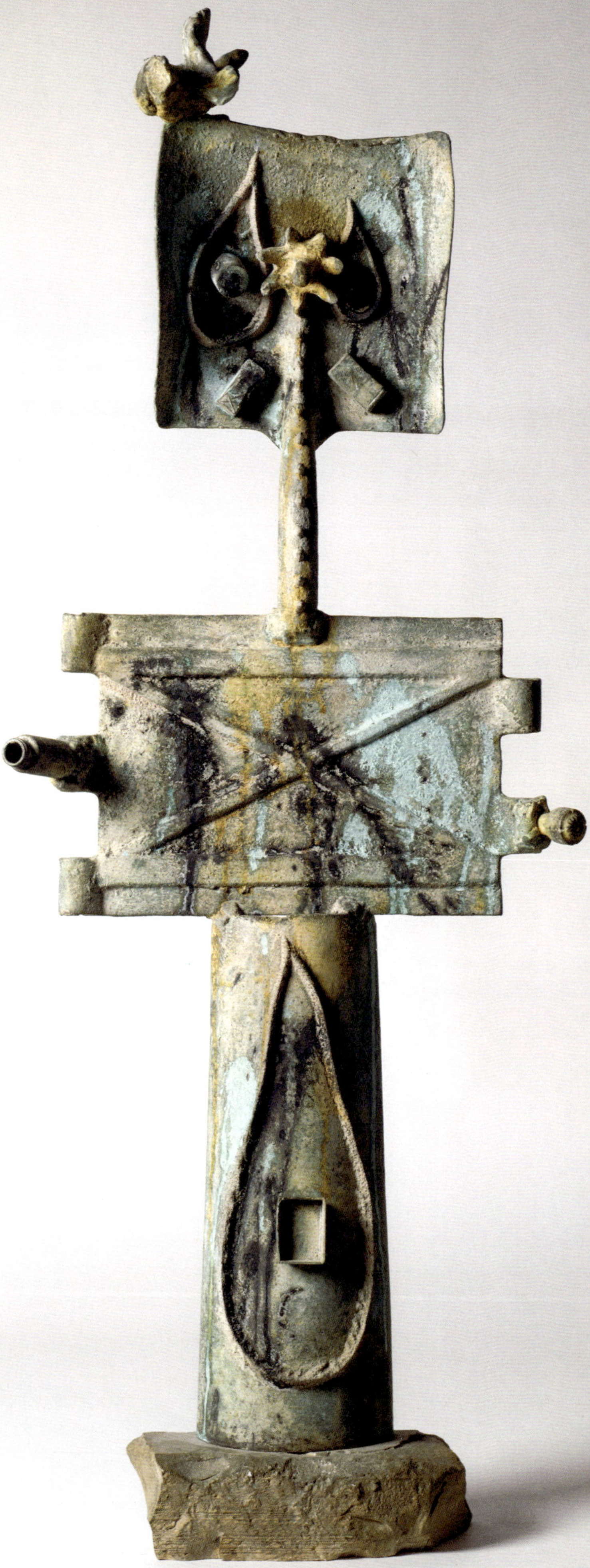

Femme et oiseau (Woman and Bird), 1970, patinated bronze, 48 1/16 × 18 7/8 × 5 1/8 in. (122 × 48 × 13 cm)

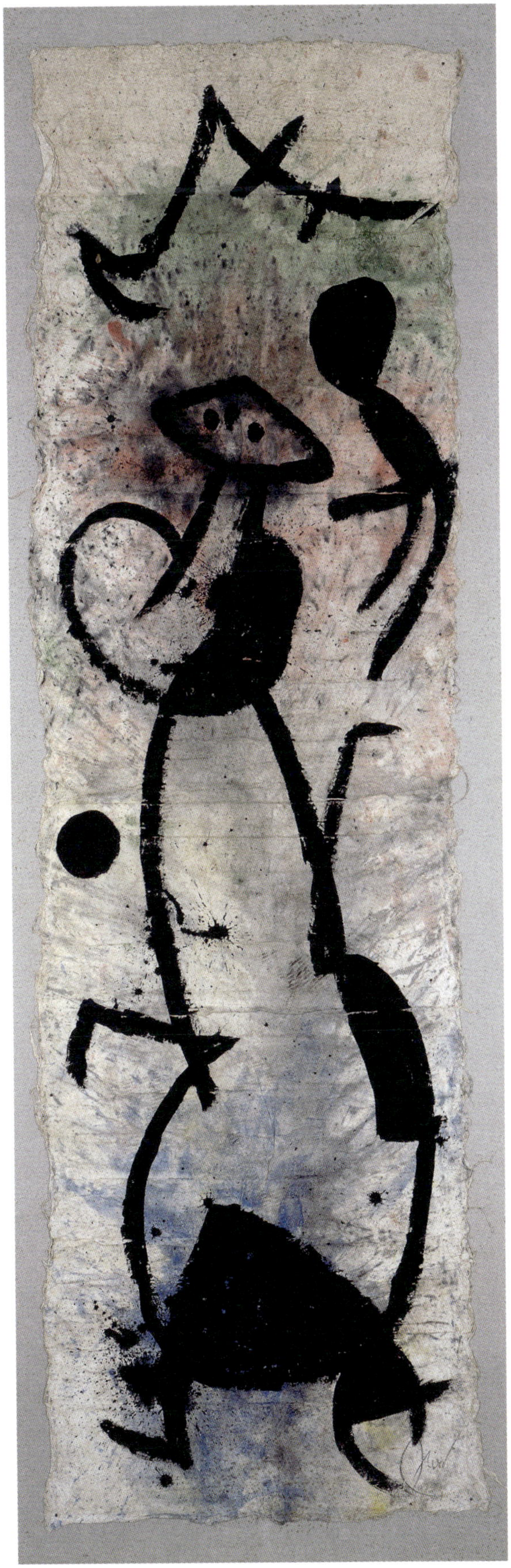

Femme oiseau (Woman Bird), 1978, ink and oil on handmade paper, 82 11/16 × 24 7/16 in. (210 × 62 cm)

Tête, oiseau (Head, Bird), 1977, india ink, lithographic ink, tempera, and wax on paper, 39⅜ × 27⅜ in. (100 × 69.5 cm)

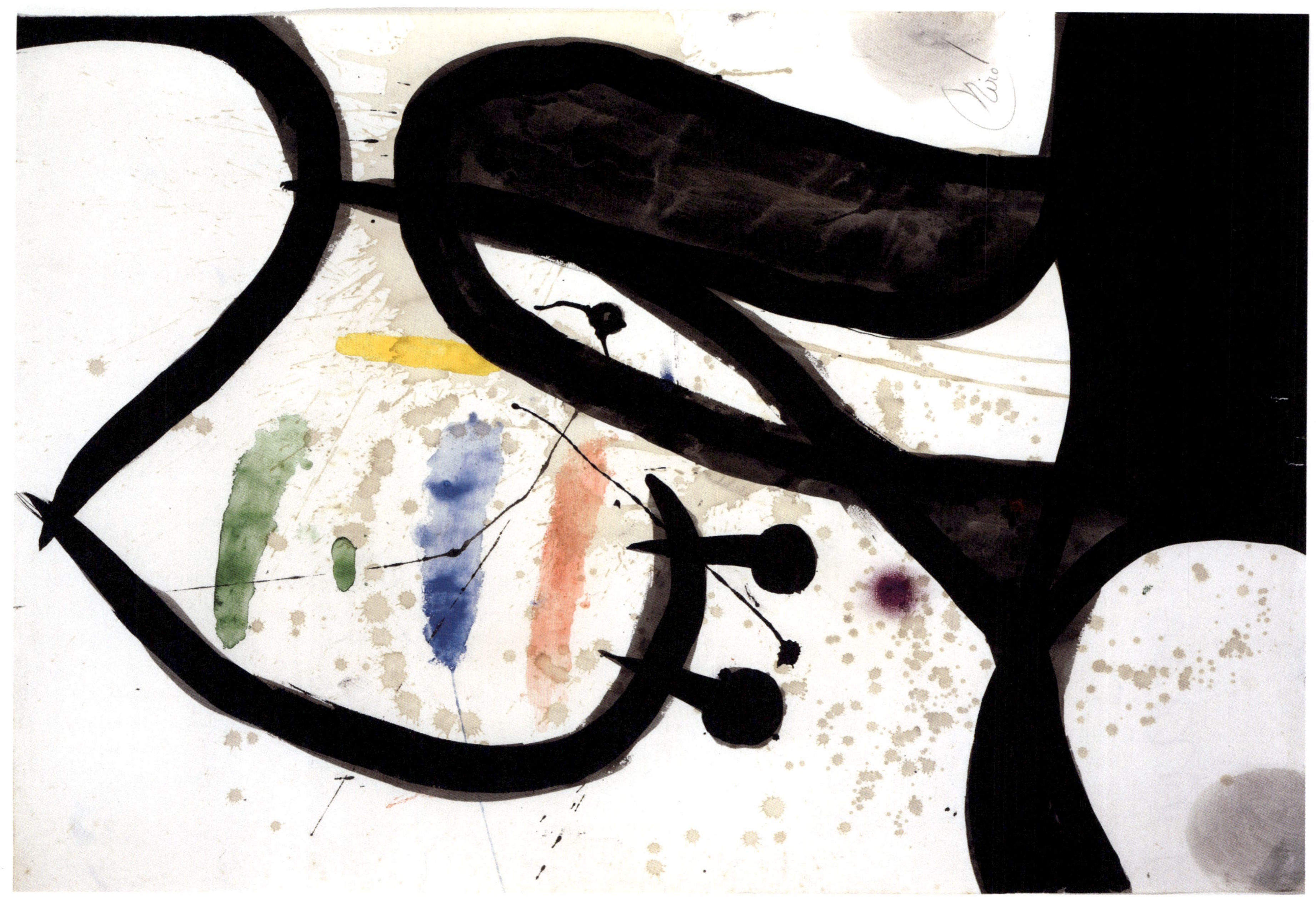

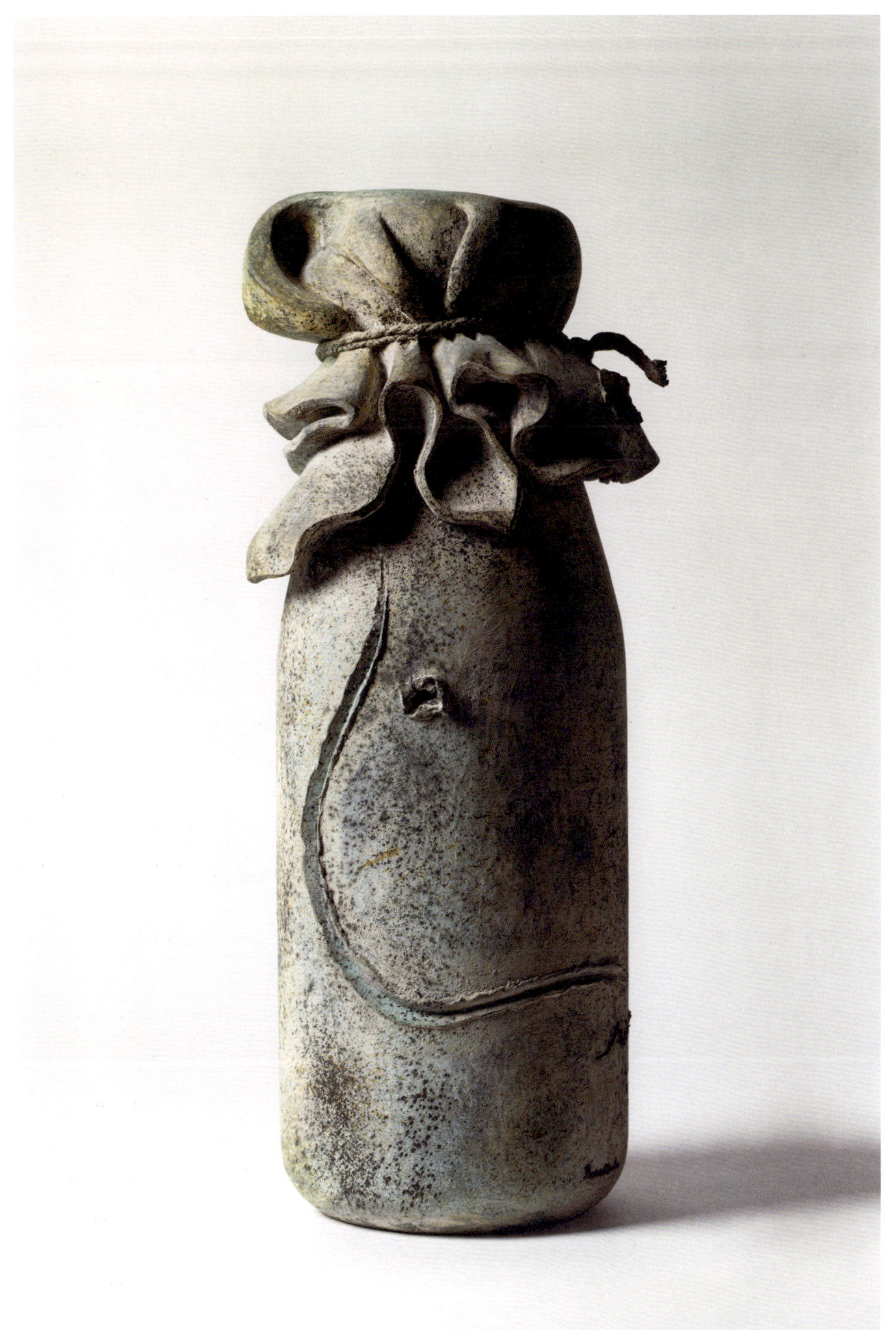

Figure, 1981, patinated bronze, 22⅝ × 10 1/16 × 9 7/16 in. (57.5 × 25.5 × 24 cm)

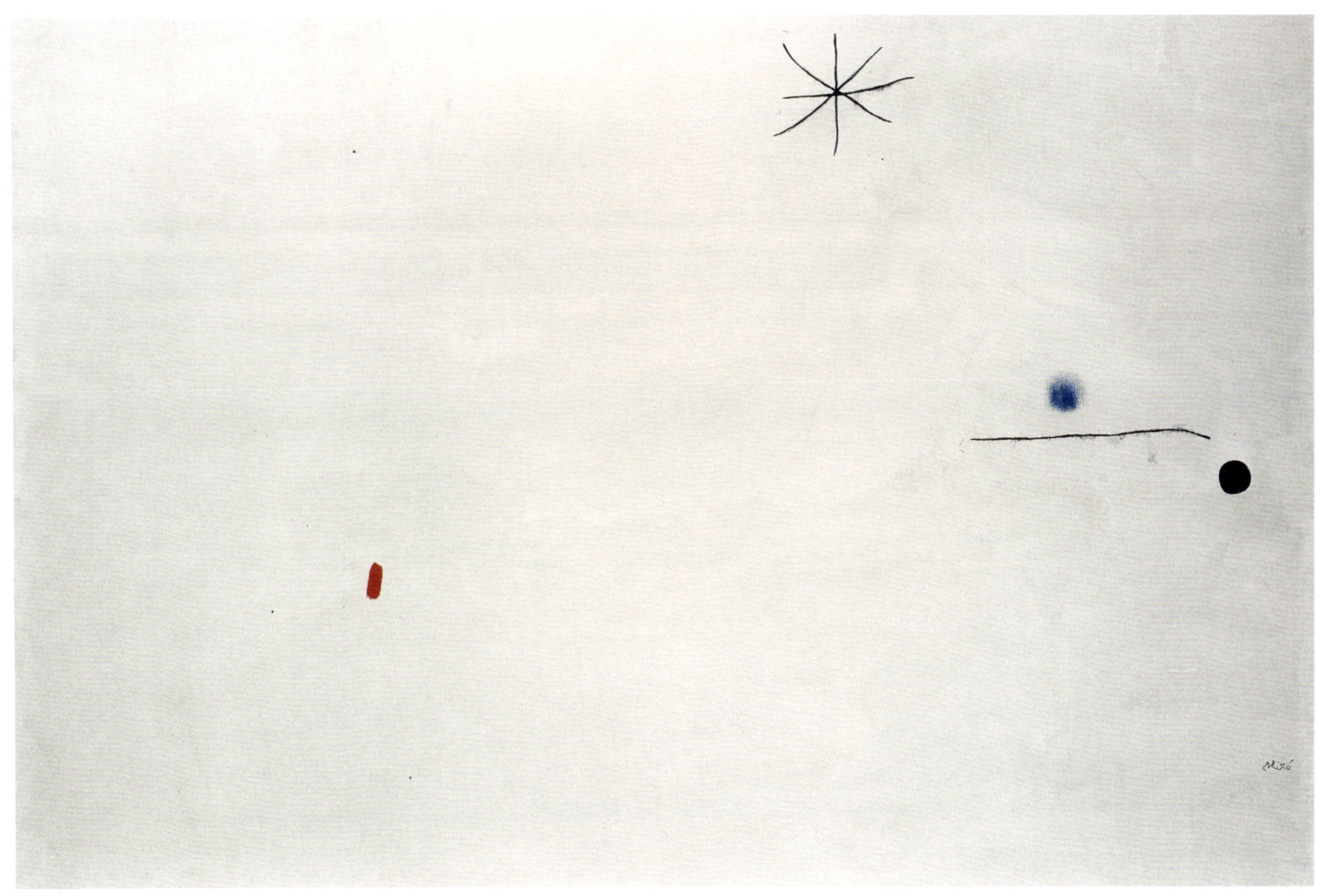

Paysage (Landscape), 1976, wax and acrylic on primed canvas, 51³⁄₁₆ × 76⅜ in. (130 × 194 cm)

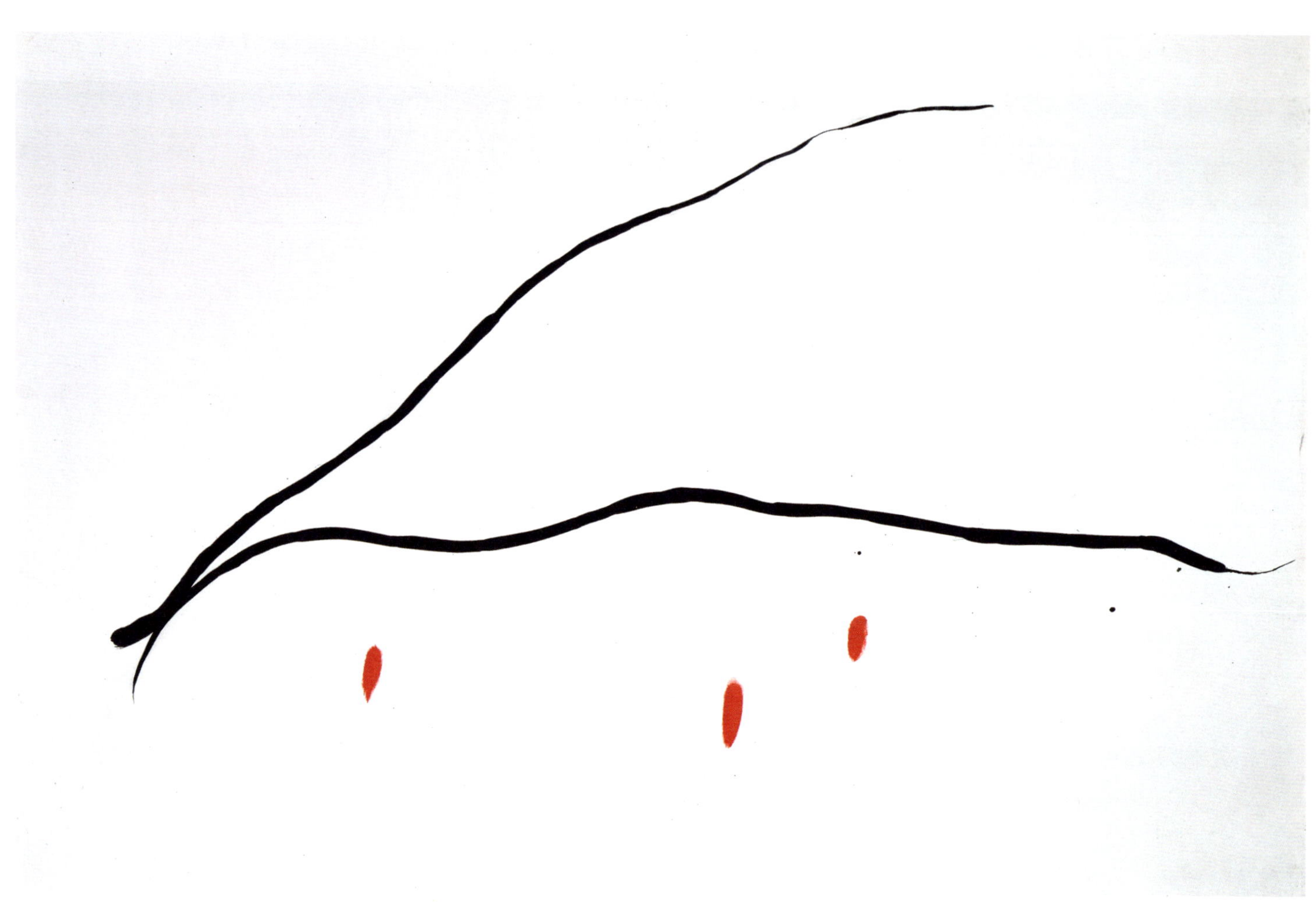

La danse des coquelicots (The Dance of the Poppies), 1973, acrylic on canvas, 51 3/16 × 76 3/4 in. (130 × 195 cm)

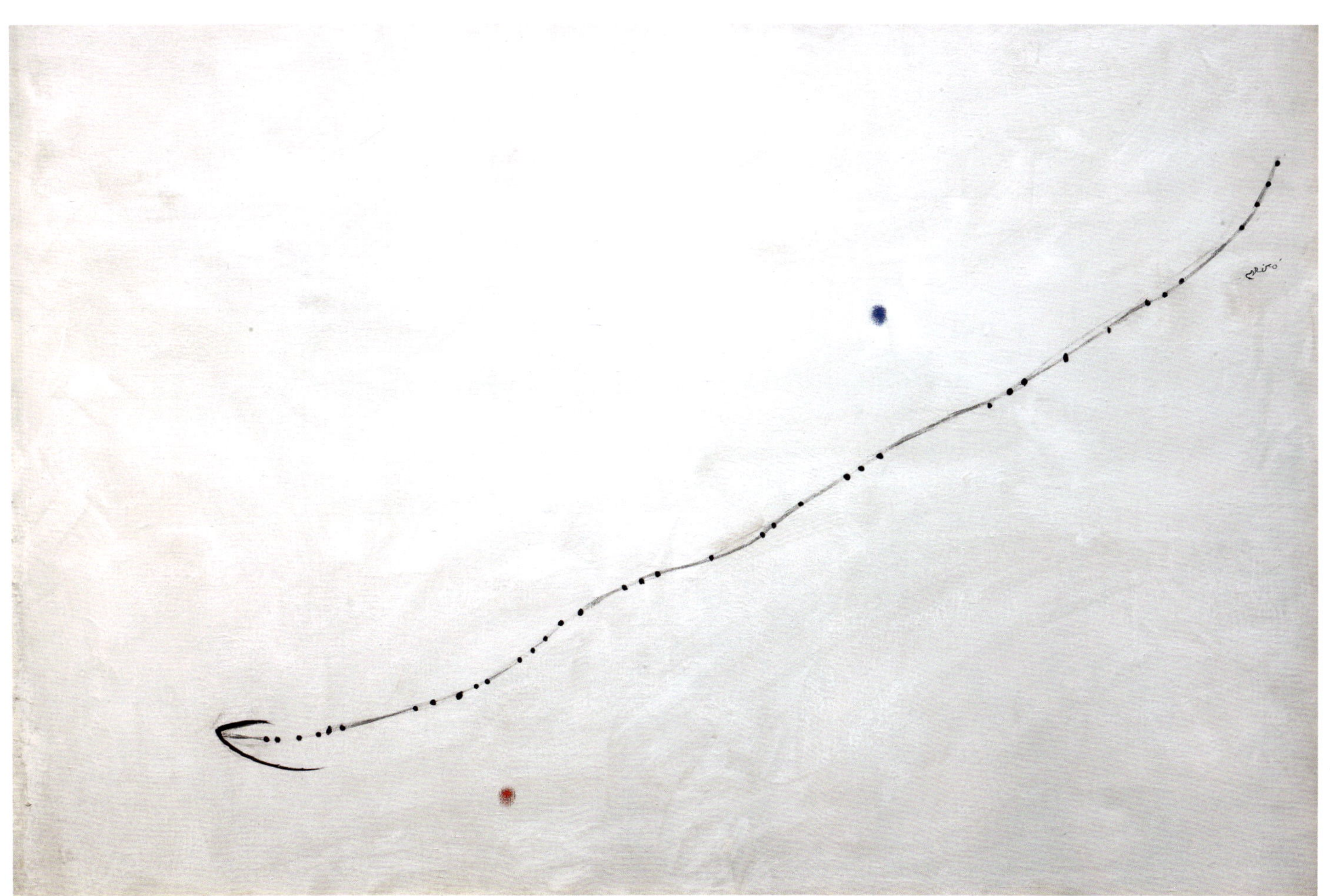

Oiseau dans l'espace (Bird in Space), 1976, acrylic on primed canvas, $51\frac{3}{16} \times 76\frac{3}{16}$ in. (130 × 193.5 cm). Detail on pp. 82–83.

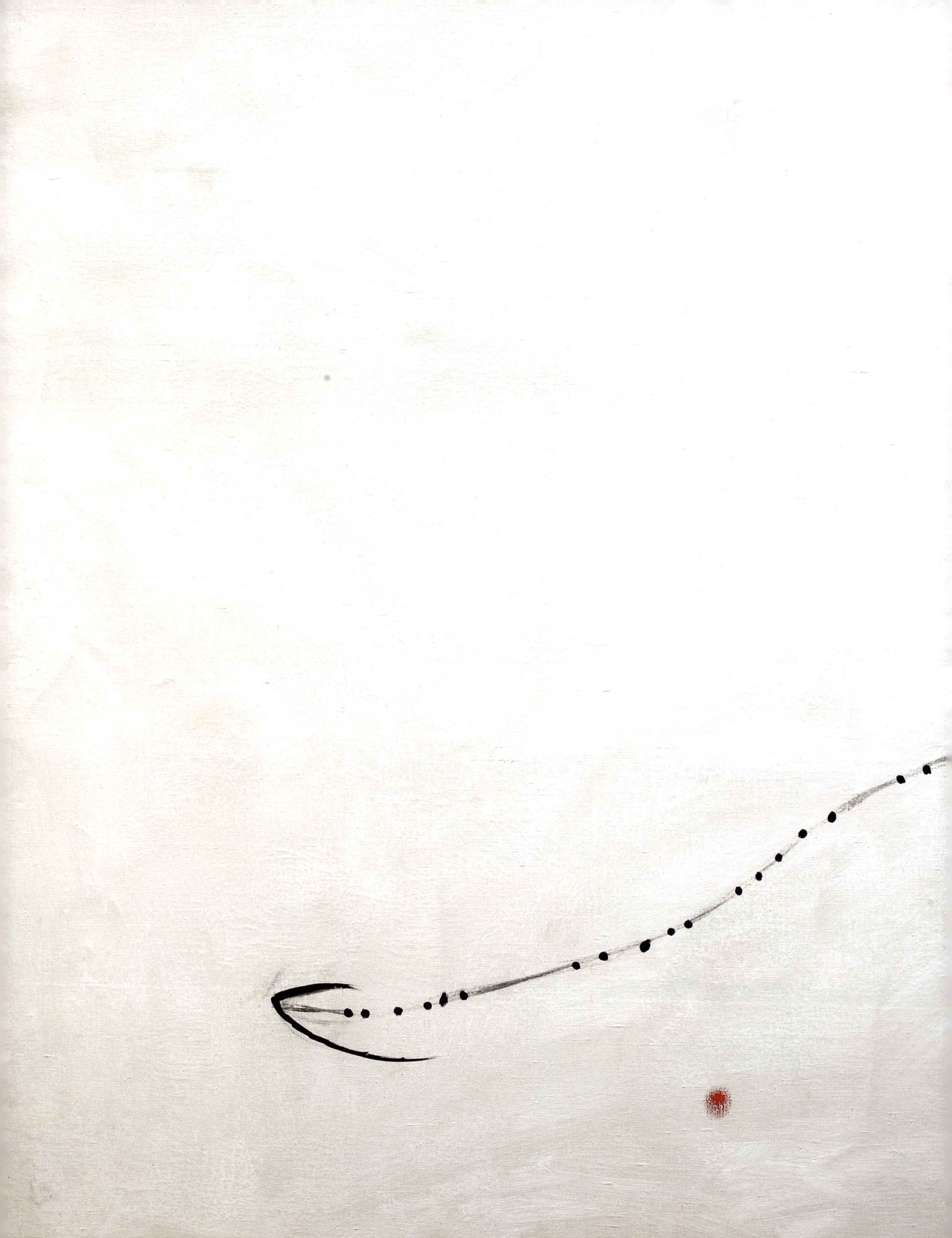

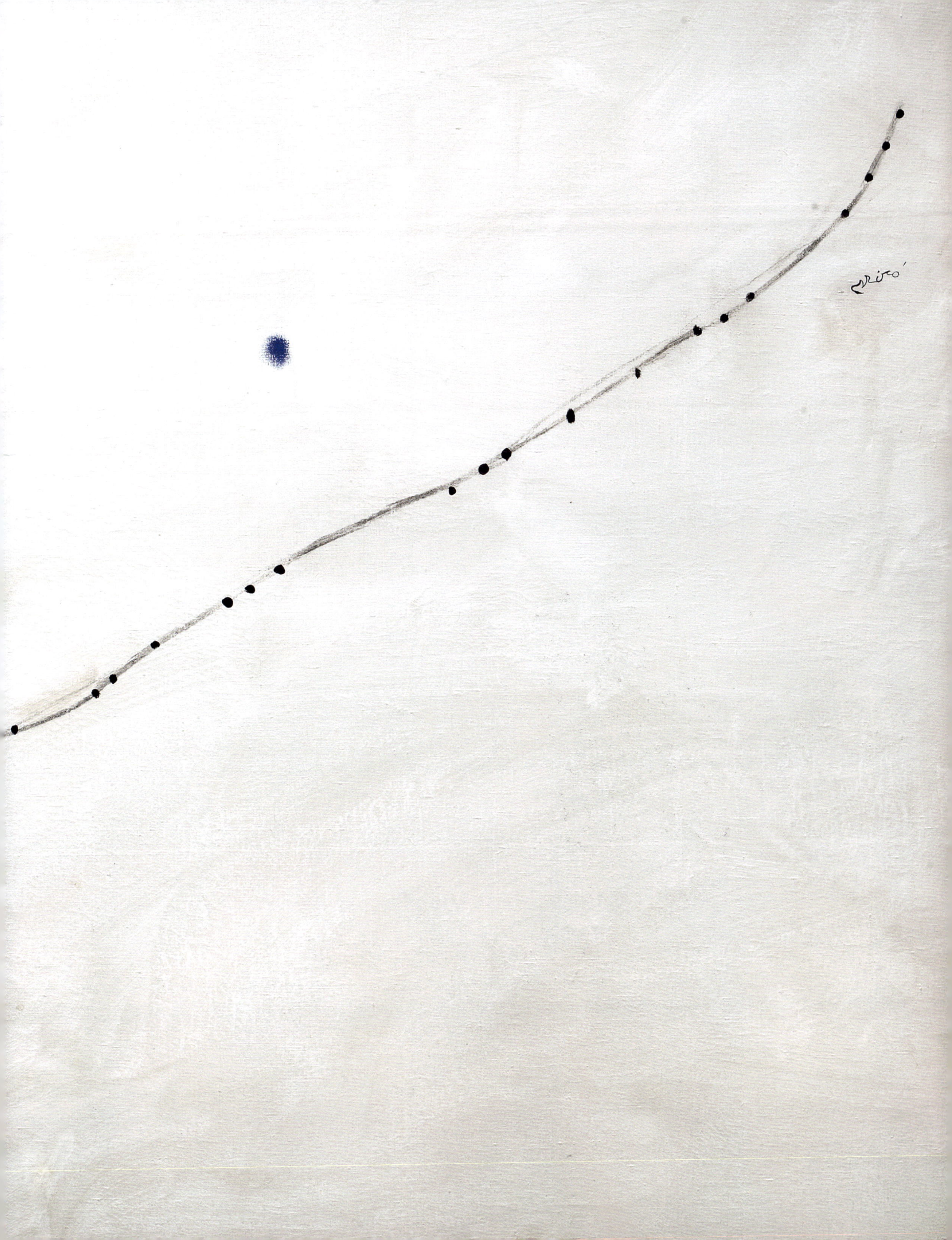
Miró

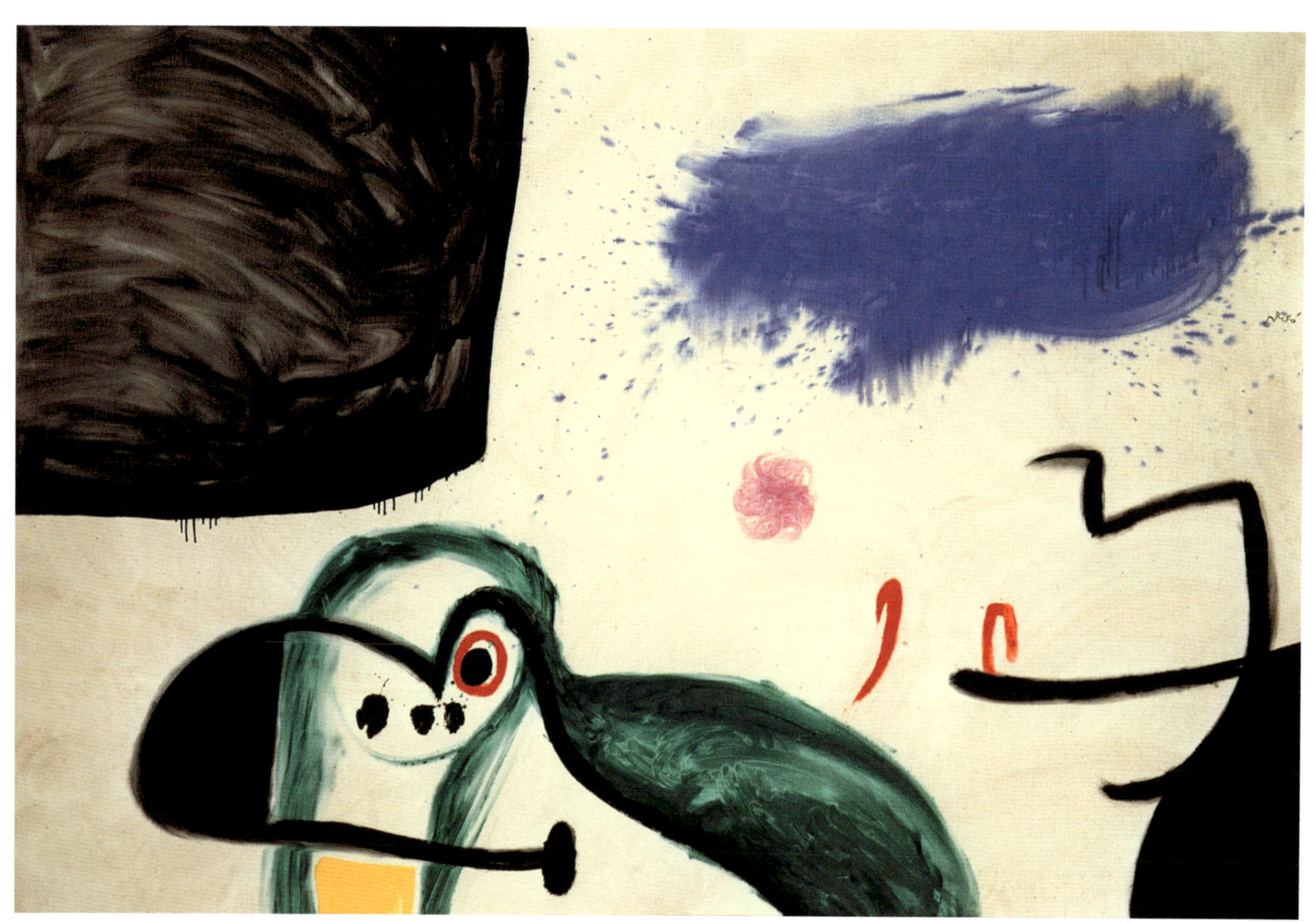

Paysage (Landscape), 1976, oil and acrylic on canvas, $51\frac{3}{16} \times 76\frac{3}{4}$ in. (130 × 195 cm)

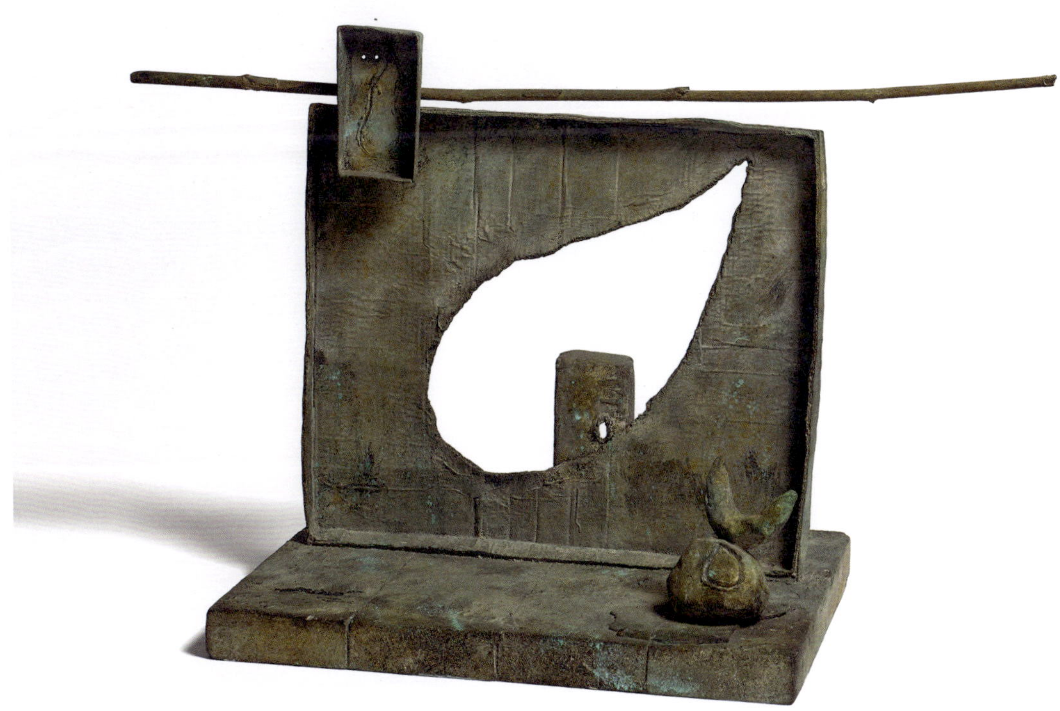

Femme sur la place d'un cimetière (Woman at the Square in a Cemetery), 1981, patinated bronze, 23¹³⁄₁₆ × 23¹⁄₁₆ × 20¹⁄₁₆ in. (60.5 × 58.5 × 50.9 cm), front. Back view below. Detail on pp. 86–87.

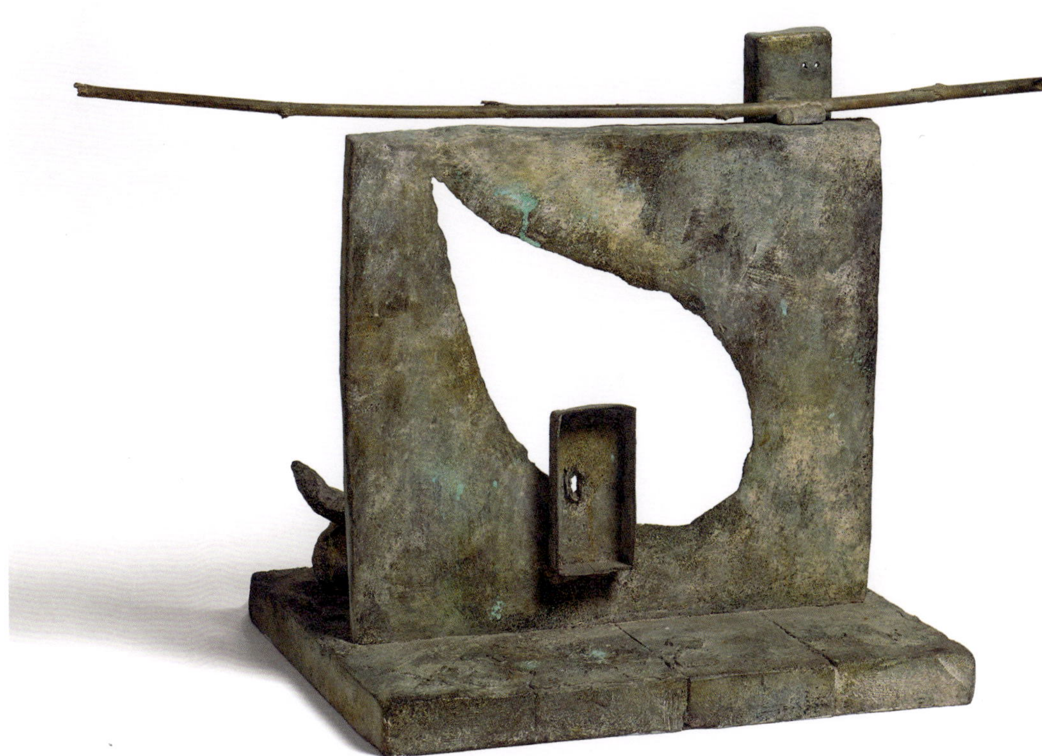

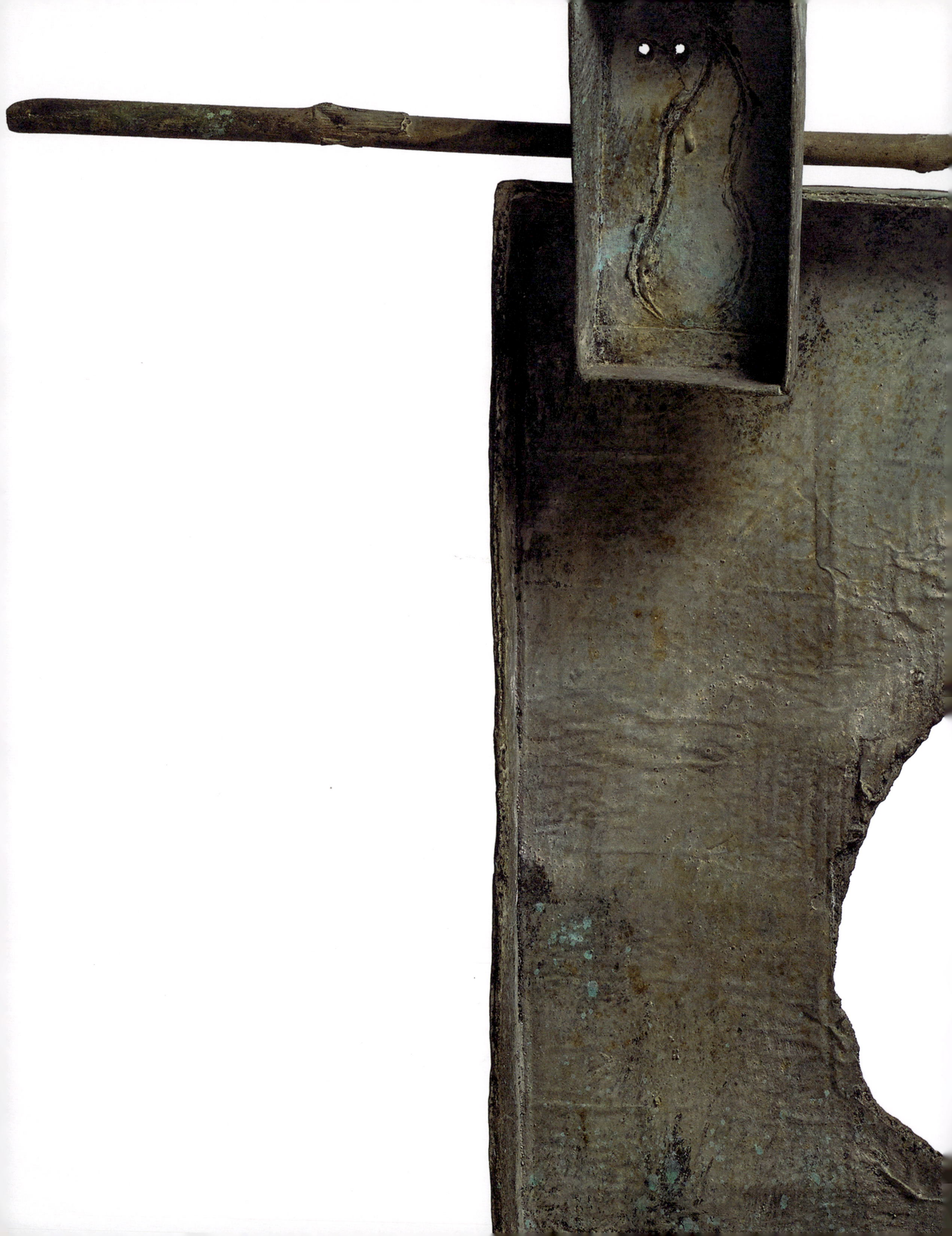

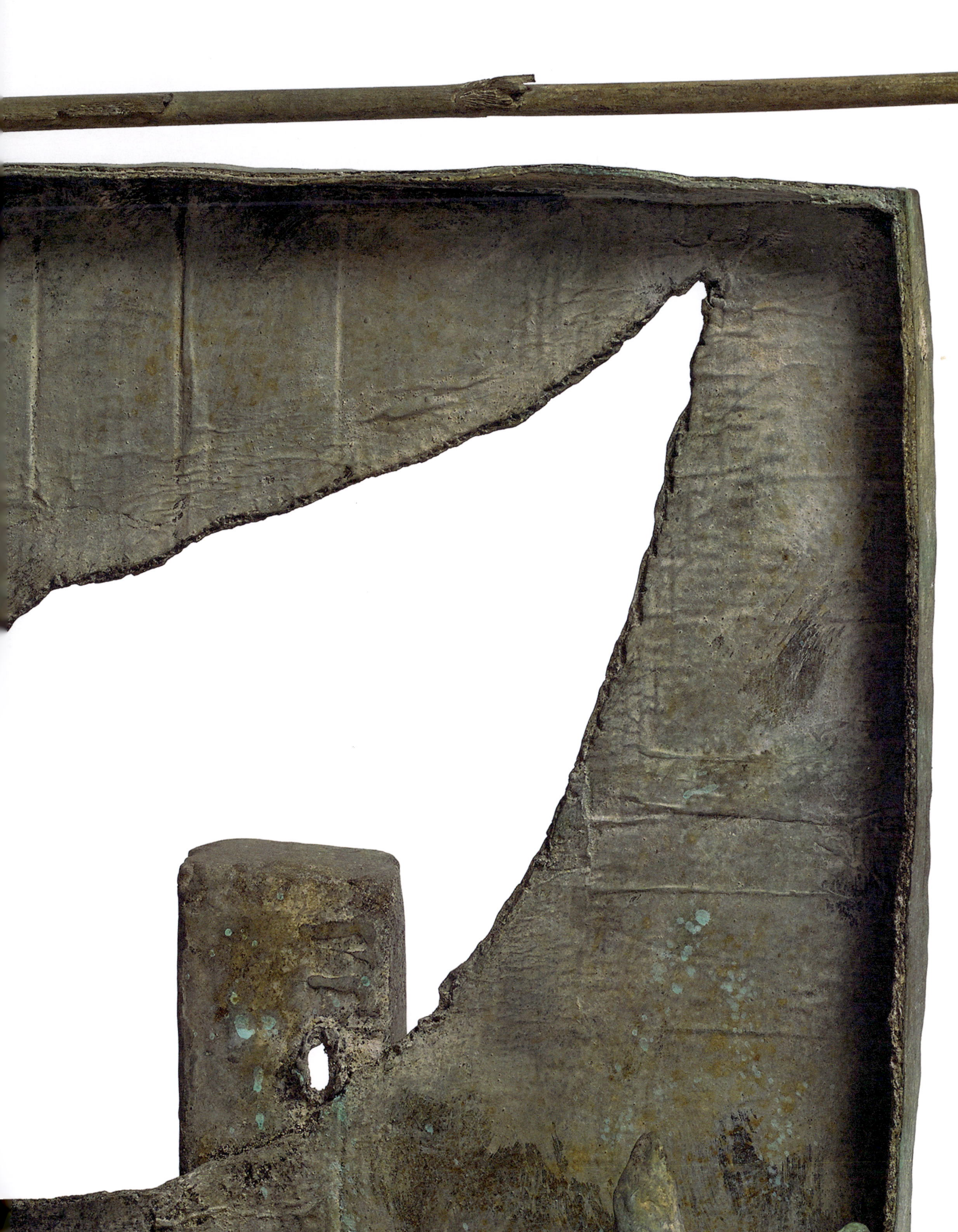

Tête et oiseau (Head and Bird), 1981, patinated bronze, 25 9/16 × 16 9/16 × 7 5/16 in. (65 × 42 × 18.5 cm)

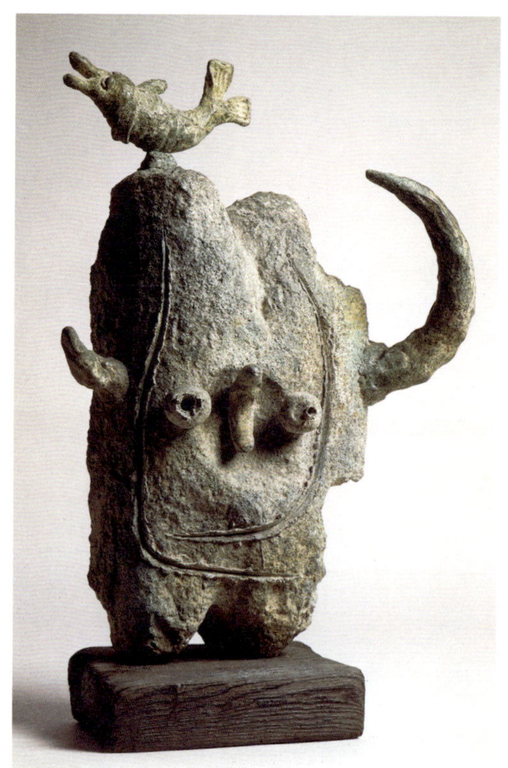

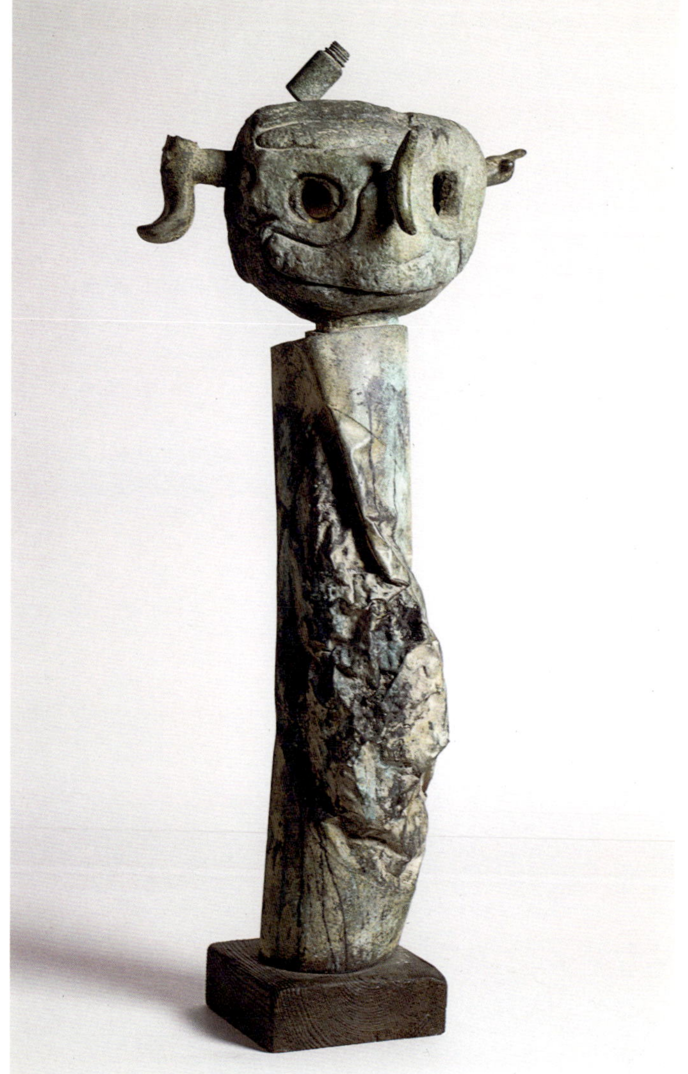

Figure, 1981, patinated bronze, 42 1/2 × 18 1/2 × 12 3/16 in. (108 × 47 × 31 cm)

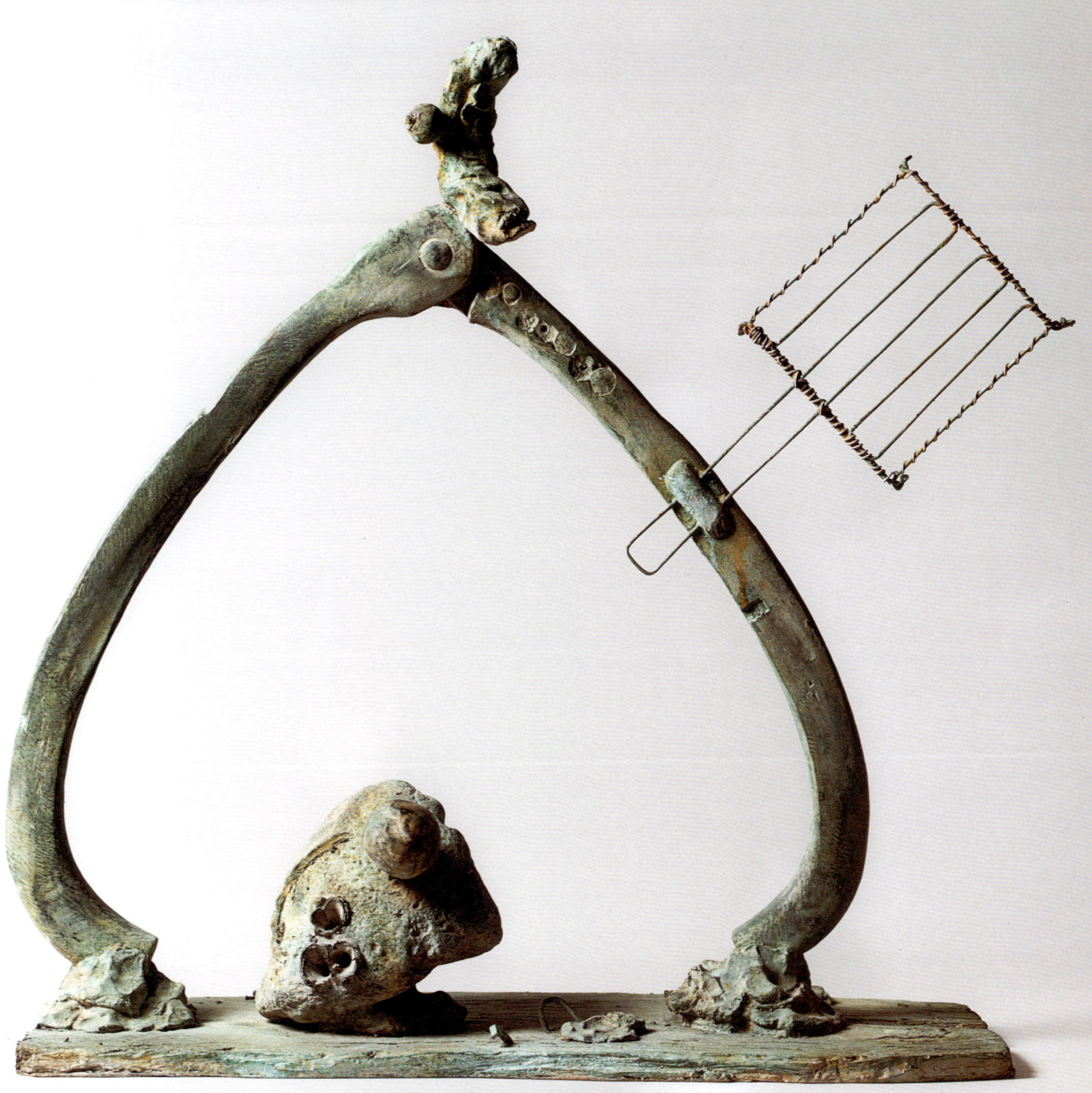

Oiseau sur une branche (Bird on a Branch), 1981, patinated bronze, 30⁵⁄₁₆ × 33¼ × 11⅝ in. (77 × 84.5 × 29 cm)